THE OPEN-HEARTH COOK-BOOK

T0149869

Gigi Nielowocki

The Author's cooking hearth

The Open-Hearth
COOKBOOK

REVISED EDITION

*Recapturing the Flavor
of Early America*

by

Suzanne Goldenson

with Doris Simpson

Alan C. Hood & Company, Inc.
CHAMBERSBURG, PENNSYLVANIA

ISBN: 0-911469-26-5
ISBN-13: 978-0-911469-26-4

Published by Alan C. Hood & Co., Inc.
Chambersburg, PA 17201

www.hoodbooks.com

Copies of *The Open-Hearth Cookbook* may be obtained by sending $18.50 per copy to:

Alan C. Hood & Co., Inc.
P.O. Box 775, Chambersburg, PA 17201

Price includes postage and handling.
Quantity discounts are available to dealers and non-profit organizations.
Write on letterhead for details.

Cover photo courtesy of Old Sturbridge Village, Sturbridge, MA

Cover and text design by James F. Brisson

Library of Congress Cataloging-in-Publication Data

Goldenson, Suzanne, 1944-
 The open-hearth cookbook : recapturing the flavor of early America / by Suzanne Goldenson with Doris Simpson.-- Rev. ed.
  p. cm.
 ISBN 0-911469-26-5 (paperback)
 1. Fireplace cookery.   2. Fireplaces. I. Simpson, Doris, 1926- II. Title
TX840.F5G63 2005
641.5'.8--dc22

2005045631

10   9   8   7   6   5   4

Contents

Preface

We first became interested in writing a book on fireplace cooking in the fall of 1979 during Thanksgiving in the Country weekend–a local house tour and fund-raiser held every year in our rural community of Sergeantsville, New Jersey. Doris Simpson and I were demonstrating our skills for the touring groups, hers being open-hearth cooking, mine, pottery. In the course of the day, we realized that we shared a common interest, collecting and using antique cooking implements. Doris was the owner and chef of a well-known local restaurant, Muirhead, and she has studied, lectured, and demonstrated extensively on the history and preparation of early American food, I, at that point, was only an inveterate collector of antiques, a fairly serious cook, and the owner of a large pre-Revolutionary walk-in cooking hearth that I was eager to put to use. Thus began our collaboration and a winter of cooking sessions that grew into this book.

While the lure and lore of old cookbooks and antique pots and other implements, and the history of how early American cooks prepared their meals at the hearth, continued to absorb and fascinate us throughout the preliminary planning and testing stages of this book, we decided to go beyond these curiosities and anachronisms and focus on how to adapt what we had learned of early cooking to the resources and tastes of the twenty-first century. Although steeped in history, the following pages are intended to be a practical guide, serving to demonstrate the mystique and pleasures of fireplace cooking for readers, and bring the best of this cooking to their tables.

Although the appeal of this subject to history buffs and food historians is obvious, why, many people ask, in this age of modern conveniences, write a book for the general public about the lost, and–to some–best forgotten art of fireplace cooking? Cooking over a wood fire is bound to be more work than cooking with modern appliances. A fire is surely not as reliable or predictable a source of heat as electricity and gas, and the resulting food, it is commonly feared, is likely to be improperly cooked and unimaginably strange-tasting.

Many answers spring to our minds when these questions are raised. Most important, we insist, is that food cooked in a fireplace tastes marvelous, *better* than food cooked in most conventional ways today—the charcoal barbecue included. And with a few minor exceptions—large cakes, soufflés, and other delicate confections—most anything one could desire to eat can be easily prepared in a fireplace. Fireplace cooking is also not difficult, and will require surprisingly few new pieces of cooking gear and few new skills of the would-be open-hearth cook. Also, as a word of encouragement, while the process of cooking over a wood fire seems alien to most modern Americans (especially those who have never camped), it is the common method, today, in many other parts of the world. Pierre Franey, one of the best-known food writers and cooks today, who grew up in a provincial part of France, commented in *Craig Claiborne's Favorites From the New York Times,* published in 1975 by the New York Times Book Co., that: "I was twelve years old before I knew people cooked in any other way."

Fireplace cooking should also be attractive in light of the growing concern and interest in energy conservation in America. As of 1978, there were 25 million fireplaces and woodburning stoves in the United States, with sales up 30 percent since the beginning of the energy crisis marked by the Arab oil embargo in 1973.* In light of this trend of wood replacing fossil fuels for heating homes, the concept of using this fuel for cooking while it warms you is likely to be an idea of more than passing merit. The vision of a pot of soup simmering at your hearth as you relax in a nearby armchair reading the Sunday paper is not only an inviting one, but a practical one, too. Certainly it is a more attractive and convenient notion, than that of a pot of stew bubbling away on the top of your oil burner!

Granted, in all honesty, if pressed, we'd have to admit that fireplace cooking has its limitations. Cooking in a fireplace does involve more work than meal preparation with modern appliances. But this is primarily because most fireplaces today are not installed in the kitchen of the house where all of the cooking paraphernalia and ingredients are stored. With careful planning, the inconvenience of trips back and forth for mixing bowls, wooden spoons, salt and pepper, and other supplies, can be kept to a minimum in a fireplace cooking session. Fireplace cooking may also seem awkward at first in other ways; and temperature control, especially, may take a little practice. We hope the pointers that follow will take most of the bugs and potential failures out of

---

Statistics from the Fireplace Institute of America

these areas for you. Fireplace cooking is also a seasonal activity, not one, except in an emergency, that one would care to pursue in July. And cooking dinner for thirty in a fireplace, however well appointed, is not a realistic idea.

But, we have found, the fun of fireplace cooking more than compensates for these drawbacks. Family and friends really seem to enjoy the experience and flavor of dinner cooked at the fireplace. And even men who would not be found within miles of their own kitchens have been seen lending a helping hand around our hearth. Add to this the practical appeal of energy conservation, and fireplace cooking emerges as an idea, to re-coin the phrase, whose time has "re-arrived."

Before we lead you step by step through the how-tos of fireplace cooking, we would like to acknowledge our indebtedness to many early America cooks who preceded us, for without them we could not have written this book. Not only did they give us hints and clues in their recipes as to how they cooked in their fireplaces, they also gave us the courage to try many cooking techniques we never would have thought could be easily performed at the hearth. For, if baking cakes in a Dutch oven was a frequent task for the early American housewife, her twenty-first-century counterparts were not to be outdone. Although we consulted many old cookbooks, we are especially grateful to the following authors: Eliza Leslie, *Directions for Cookery in its Various Branches* (1848); Hannah Glasse, *The Art of Cookery Made Plain and Easy* (1796); Amelia Simmons (author of the first wholly American cookbook), *American Cookery* (1796); Susannah Carter, *The Frugal Colonial Housewife* (1772); And Mary Randolph, *The Virginia Housewife* (1885).

We would also like to thank my husband, Dan and Barbara Morrison who read and commented on much of the material in its preliminary stages; both our families, who sampled and provided helpful criticism of the fireplace fare (the cornmeal biscuits with bacon included in Chapter 7 were my seven-year-old son, Andy's, favorite); Rosalie Santosuosso for typing the completed manuscript; and especially my two helpers, Violet Veseulko and Dorothy Jackson, who provided substitute mothering for my two children so that I could have the time and the peace of mind to write.

Suzanne Goldenson
Cambridge, Massachusetts
September 2005

To: Beverly Jones, who introduced us
And to
"Thanksgiving In the Country,"
which provided the inspiration

Fireplace in the 1840 kitchen at Indian Dormitory, Mackinac Island, Michigan.

1

Getting Started: The Fireplace, An Inventory of Its Cooking Implements and Their Care

The Cooking Hearth

For nearly two hundred years before the first cookstoves came into use in the early 1800s, American cooks prepared all their meals in the fireplace. In the earliest New England settlements, these first cooking fireplaces were nothing more than crude open circular hearths placed in the center of a one-room dwelling. A hole overhead in the thatched roof permitted smoke to escape. Later, the design of these fireplaces was improved by bringing the chimney down from the roof to form a hood over the fire to direct the smoke upwards and out. To the hood, sides were then added that enclosed the chimney on three sides, creating the precursor of the modern fireplace. In these early fireplaces, the hearth (fireplace floor) was usually made of field stones, irregularly patched together with mud. The chimneys were built of "catted" logs (logs bonded with plaster, sometimes called "cat" or clay) and lined with clay. They were very flammable, and because of frequent fires, the use of these materials in fireplace construction was quickly banned. The logs and mud were then replaced by more substantial and durable materials: stone (usually quarried granite) and bricks held together by mortar made from natural lime deposits or pulverized seashells. From these basic materials the first real fireplaces as we know them today were constructed, and many of them are still standing.

The fireplace, from this point on, underwent many changes in design during its reign as sole source of warmth and cooking heat in American homes. In some early American dwellings, the first fireplaces were located off a central

1

chimney in the middle of the house with outlets in each of the rooms. This arrangement may have become popular to avoid taxes, since a chimney tax levied on homeowners was based on the number of chimneys in a house, and not on the number of fireplaces it contained. But a more common location for the fireplace was against an outside wall. This was especially true of the kitchen fireplace.

The kitchen was the heart of the colonial home, and its fireplace reflected this. It was enormous when compared with fireplaces installed in homes today, usually at least eight, and sometimes as much as ten feet wide. It was deep as well, often accommodating a settle bench on an inside wall where family members huddled to keep warm on freezing winter evenings. These first cavernous fireplaces had no dampers. Their jambs (side walls) and back walls were built perpendicular to one another, giving the fireplace opening a boxy shape hearkening back to the design of European fireplaces of medieval times.

In the homes of more affluent families, these fireplaces frequently had a brick bake oven built into the back wall of the fireplace, either to the right or to the left of the smoke channel. The earliest of these bake ovens shared the central flue with the main fireplace. To heat them, a fire was built directly on the oven floor; the oven door was kept open to provide oxygen and to allow the smoke to escape up the central chimney flue. Later, bake ovens were

Stone, wattle, and daub fireplace, Plimoth Plantation, Plymouth, Massachusetts, circa 1627.

improved upon by the addition of a completely separate flue, or one that fed into the main chimney flue. These modifications permitted preheating the oven with its door closed. This was a design change that not only speeded up the preheating process by cutting down on heat loss from the oven, but which also cut down on the consumption of firewood, a commodity which became scarce as time went on in the more densely populated regions. These fireplace ovens were widely called beehive ovens since their baking chambers which extended behind or alongside the fireplace, were dome-shaped, like a bee's nest.

The lintel or mantel support on the first cooking hearths was generally a hefty wooden beam, but sometimes granite was used. These supports did not become decorative, or even intentionally useful, elements in fireplace construction until a later period. That some of these supports protruded slightly and became used as a shelf to hold plates and other household items seems at first to have been incidental. These first cooking fireplaces were also frequently whitewashed to improve their reflecting abilities and to make them more attractive. Because of their immense proportions, and because the cook had to step into the fireplace opening to use her bake oven or to warm up on the settle bench, they have become known as walk-in fireplaces.

As craftsmen and homeowners became more skilled and experienced, fireplace construction in America improved. By the mid-eighteenth century, the bake oven was located on a front side wall of the fireplace, and its door opened into the room, instead of into the fireplace opening. Now, an ash pit was often added beneath the oven, or a chute might connect the bake oven's floor to the fireplace hearth. These features simplified the cook's job of cleaning out the ashes and remains of the fire from the oven to ready it for baking. The pit also served as a convenient storage area for ashes, which were used in making soap. Now, to preheat, load or unload her oven, the cook did not have to enter the fireplace or reach over its flames—a much safer arrangement.

With the removal of the bake oven from the brick wall of the fireplace, the fireplace opening was reduced in size and modified in design. These changes improved its efficiency for heating the room as it cooked dinner. One such refinement was to curve the bricks on its back wall increasingly inward as they rose from the flu, thus directing heat back into the room instead of sending it right up the chimney. Other sophisticated design elements were added, and the proportion between the chimney height and size and the fireplace opening were studied to increase the heating abilities of the fireplace still further, and to prevent it from smoking, a problem on windy days. The men most responsible for these improvements were two Americans, one famous and the other infamous: Benjamin Franklin and Count Rumford (Sir Benjamin Thompson).

Paired fireplaces in the Moravian Tavern, Old Salem, Winston-Salem, North Carolina, circa 1784. The left one was used for baking and washing, the one on the right for cooking with a weight-driven spit.

Benjamin Franklin became so absorbed with the topic of reducing smoke from fireplaces that his observations led to the invention of the damper, and then of the first woodstoves. Count Rumford, a notorious Tory who had to flee this country, focused his attention solely on the fireplace. He refined its design to such a degree that he developed a model of exceptional efficiency, which was practically smokeless. Unfortunately it required considerable skill to build a Rumford fireplace. For this reason, and because his studies coincided with the introduction of the rapidly accepted woodstove, Rumford's concepts were never widely put into use in the Colonial and post-Revolutionary periods. But the Rumford model is very much the standard for modern stone masons.

Kitchen fireplaces also had other special modifications and features which made them particularly suitable for cooking. A central feature of the cooking hearth was its crane. The crane was a large iron bracket hinged to the fireplace jamb. From S hooks and trammels placed on it, the cook suspended her cooking pots over the fire. The crane's hinges allowed her to swing it like a gate, on and off the fire, to season the soup and generally attend to her cooking food without scorching her face, getting smoke in her eyes, or reaching over the fire.

But the American housewife didn't always have this convenience. Until the eighteenth century iron was scarce, and cranes were preceded in cooking fireplaces by lugpoles. The lugpole, also called a lugstick and backbar, consisted essentially of a sturdy, very green, sapling (beech and maple were preferred) which rested on the projecting inner ledges of the fireplace throat six or seven feet above the hearth. Great care was taken to replace the lugpole before it became charred, since if it broke, it might not only spill the soup or stew, but scald the cook or child sitting before the fire. (Death or maiming by fire and scalding water took a toll of Colonial cooks second only to death in childbirth.) Because of this ever-present hazard, and because it was very difficult for the cook to lift her heavy iron pots on and off the pothooks that attached them to the lugpole, they were readily replaced with the iron crane as soon as possible.

Also, with the greater availability of iron came the introduction of a proper iron door hinged to the brickwork of the beehive oven. These replaced the fitted wooden slab or bricks which were previously pushed into place or stacked to seal the oven on baking day.

In the 1800s, firebacks or fireplates also came into use. These were thick decorative iron slabs, sometimes incorporating an allegorical or biblical motif, or a family's coat of arms. They were set into the back walls of the fireplace and protected its masonry from the intense heat of the ever-present cooking fire, which caused deterioration of the bricks and mortar. Another practical, although minor, feature of the firebacks was that they reflected some of the fire's heat back into the room.

While the standard evolution and design of most kitchen fireplaces in America followed the preceding pattern, many early cooking hearths departed from this outline. Fireplaces reflected the imagination, ethnic origins, and resourcefulness of regional masons and home craftsmen in America. One such interesting variation in fireplace design, the cooking fireplace in General Varnum's Quarters, an eighteenth-century farmhouse in Valley Forge, Pennsylvania, is an inglenook. A Welsh custom, an inglenook is a small window or opening built into the rear wall of the fireplace. It let in additional daylight and gave the cook a glimpse of the outside world, perhaps helping to relieve the tedium of the long hours spent by the fire. (The inglenook was the first window over the kitchen sink.) There were many other fireplace variations. In the Moravian Tavern, Old Salem, Winston-Salem, North Carolina, built in 1784, the kitchen contains a pair of matching arched fireplaces. One hearth was used for brick-oven baking and washing, the other for cooking. In the South, fireplaces frequently had auxiliary cooking "counters." The Hermann Grima House kitchen in New Orleans has an example of this type of fireplace construction. Cooking counters were raised brick surfaces about waist high, many times tiled, under which a fire was built. The cook placed her pots over the circular openings in the counter, called stew holes, to heat her food. Another traditional Southern practice, especially on big plantations, was to have a separate "summer" kitchen, or to locate the kitchen away from the central living areas of the house, in its own wing. Not only was this a safety measure in light of the frequency of fires, but setting the kitchen apart kept the main house cooler during the summer months, which were particularly hot in this part of the country.

Early American Cooking Implements

At the height of the fireplace cooking era, in addition to the standard fire-tending tools—shovels, pokers, tongs, and bellows—cooks had a wonderfully innovative and versatile assortment of cooking implements and pots at their disposal. Among this impressive array, which festooned the hearth, were peels, posnets, spiders, bird ovens, coffee-roasters, tilting teakettles, ember tongs, salamanders, tin kitchens, Dutch ovens, clock jacks, griddles, waffle irons, wafer irons, spits of all lengths, and kettles of all sizes.

Of course, the kitchen fireplaces in the earliest households did not display this rich variety of accessories. In the 1600s, John Winthrop wrote to his wife to bring to Massachusetts Bay to equip her kitchen only "2 or 3 skillets of several sizes, a large frying pan, a small stewing pan, and a can to boil a pudding in…" this gives a striking example of how little the fireplace cook could manage to get along with. An inventory of the furnishings in an average early American kitchen of a slightly later period was equally modest. It probably would have included an iron pot, a kettle, a large frying pan, gridiron, a skillet or two, and a supply of wooden tableware, called "treenware." The treenware usually consisted of common eating platters (trenchers), dishes, spoons, and primitive table knives, made from sharpened sticks. Even as the country prospered and became more populated, and more kitchen implements and pots became available to cooks, most homemakers still made do with a few items. And the lavishly decorated and well-appointed kitchens at many restorations open to the public today probably present an accurate picture of only the wealthier family hearths.

Despite the generally sparse appointments of most cooking fireplaces, cooks were still able to perform all of the basic cooking techniques with a surprisingly high degree of accuracy, and with remarkably tasty results. This was due in large part to the resourcefulness of the average homemaker. Using the wooden lid of her flour barrel as a cake sheet to bake bannocks or journey cake or for planking a fish was commonplace. Pots, which were designed for a particular cooking technique, were used in a variety of other ways as well. The common boiling vessel, usually filled with a simmering soup or stew, was sometimes inverted over a bread and heaped with ashes and hot coals to form a primitive oven. The sharp edge of the exceptionally long-handled frying pan was known to have doubled as a tool to scrape kernels off ears of corn, a preliminary step in making cornmeal, which replaced wheat flour as the staff of life in early America.

An Inventory of Fireplace Cooking Pots and Implements

Here is a list of the varied implements and pots available to the early American cook and the needs that they were primarily designed to fulfill. Descriptions of how they were used by a fireplace cook in the preparation of her daily meals, and how they can be adapted or duplicated for use today, are given in the following chapters on cooking techniques.

The inventory and diagrams that follow are not typical of what would be found in an average early American kitchen. They are intended instead to show all of the implements generally developed for the cooking fireplace and to illustrate their typical cooking position on the hearth. Two distinguishing characteristics of these pots and other implements is that many of them have three short legs and curved, overhead handles, called bails. These made them particularly suited for fireplace cooking. The feet supported the pot over a bed of glowing coals when its contents were cooking on the hearth. The curved handles allowed the cook to hang the pots and other utensils from her crane, if that was the preferred cooking location.

Andirons, cooking. These differed from common andirons in that attached to their verticals were a series of hooks to support a spitted roast. The different levels of the supports (sometimes called lugs) permitted adjustment of the distance of the roast from the fire, and thus its cooking temperature. (1)

Ash shovel. A long-handled shovel with a flat, broad end, used for removing embers and ashes from the beehive oven in preparation for baking in it. Sometimes ash shovels are confused with peels, which are wooden, since they have a similar shape, and often in a pinch ash shovels doubled for these implements. Peels, however, were used expressly for transferring breads and other food stuffs into and out of the beehive oven. When ash shovels were used as peels, their flat end was carefully cleaned first, so that no lingering ashes would get onto the food (especially foods baked without the benefit of baking pans). (2)

1. Cooking Andirons

2. Ash shovels

3. Bird oven with drip pan

4. Coffee roaster

5. Crane

6. Dangle spit

7. Doughnut kettle

8. Dutch oven

9. Ember tongs

11. Griddle

10. Frying pan

12. *Gridiron*

13. *Jack*

15. **Wooden Peels**

14. *Cooking kettle*

16. *Pot hooks*

17. *Posnet*

10

Bird oven. A small, reflecting oven with sharp hooks for impaling small song- or game birds when roasting them before the fire. (3)

Coffee roaster. A long-handled, cylindrical metal container with a pointed end for twirling coffee beans before the fire to roast them evenly. Chocolate bean roasters of a similar design were also used. (4)

Crane. A large iron bracket, hinged to one side of the fireplace, from which the cook hung her pots over the fire. It swung to and fro like a gate, facilitating the hanging, removal, and tending of the cooking food. (5)

Dangle spit. A three-pronged hook on a chain or trammel which meat was attached to for roasting. (6)

Doughnut kettle. A small, shallow, cast iron kettle with a bail used for frying doughnuts or fritters. (7)

Dutch oven. A footed, cast iron kettle with a flanged lid and a bail. Its forté was baking, which was usually carried out on the fireplace floor. But the early American cook sometimes hung this kettle from the crane, as well. (8)

Ember tongs. Scissors-like pliers used for gripping a hot ember and passing it over food to brown its top, or for lighting pipes, candles, etc. (9)

Frying pan. A shallow, flat-bottomed, long-handled pan for frying food. It sat over the coals on a specially designed trivet with a movable arm that supported its long handle. (10)

Griddle. Not all griddles were designed to hang from the crane, but most were. Griddles were used for baking biscuits, muffins, small cakes, pancakes and for general sautéing. Some of the hanging griddles had small feet so that they could stand independently on the hearth, as well. Other griddles, designed solely for use over coals on the hearth floor, usually had a single pot-like handle, rather than a bail. (11)

Gridiron. A square grill with legs and a handle used for broiling food over the coals. Gridirons also doubled as trivets for supporting pots over the glowing coals. (12)

Jacks. Mechanical devices that automatically turned the roasting food before the fire to cook it evenly. A number of different jacks were developed for fireplace use. They included: the clock jack, bottle jack, smoke jack, and steam jack. (13)

Kettle, cooking. These boiling vessels came in a variety of sizes, shapes and materials. A common type was the rounded, cast iron model with three short legs and a bail. They are frequently referred to as gypsy or sometimes bulge kettles today. Kettles were also made of other materials, such as copper, bell metal, brass, and block tin. Not all had feet, and those that did not usually had flat bottoms or a frame to stabilize their rounded bottoms and to raise them up over the coals—or they had bails (handles) to hang them over the fire. (14)

Peel. A long-handled, flat, wooden shovel with a broad, flat end used for transferring foodstuffs into and out of the beehive oven. Some of the wooden peels had shorter handles. It has been speculated that these were used for removing pies, crocks of beans, and other heavier items from the oven, since the shorter handle gave the cook more control when moving these items. (2, 15)

Pothooks. Simple, heavy wrought iron hooks for hanging implements, pots, etc. from the crane. A popular configuration for these devices was to shape them like the letter S. Hooks of this design are called S hooks. A number of S hooks could be linked together to form a chain to adjust the hanging pot's distance from the fire, and thus its cooking temperature. Pothooks in other styles were designed to fit the needs of the cook. These variations included a double-pronged version which gave pots, especially shallow ones like the doughnut kettle, extra stability when hanging from the crane. Another type of pothook acted as a lever, and allowed the cook to tilt a teakettle of hot water as it hung on the crane, and pour its contents without lifting it from the crane. (16)

Posnet. A small stewing pot or saucepan with a rounded bottom referred to in some sources as a skillet. It had a straight handle and three legs. (17)

Rotating broiler. A round, revolving wrought or cast iron grill on which the cook broiled food over the coals. It had three short legs and a straight handle. It served the same purpose as the gridiron, but its movable grilling surface gave the cook more control and more options when dealing with the broiling temperatures. (18)

Salamander. Frequently confused with the ash shoved, the true salamander was a long-handled metal device with a thick plate at one end that was preheated in the fire and used for browning off the tops of food. (19)

Skewers. Short, spear-like devices that fastened roasting meat to the spit. The skewers were pushed into the meat through holes in the spit, and then out the other side of the roast. (20)

Spider or Spyder. A shallow, black, cast iron frying pan which sat on its own splayed legs. So-called for its spider-like appearance. (21)

Spit. A long metal spear with a sharpened end that pierced the meat and supported it before the fire in a horizontal position on cooking andirons or S hooks. One end of the spit was usually articulated into a handle so that the meat could be turned easily before the fire. A variation on the standard spit was the basket spit. These had a compartment which held fragile-fleshed foods, such as fish, rather than piercing them. (22)

18. *Rotating broiler*

19. *Salamander*

20. *Skewers and holder*

21. *Spider*

22. *Spit*

23. *Teakettle*

24. *Tin kitchen*

25. *Toaster*

26. *Trammel*

27. *Trivets*

28. *Toasting fork*

29. *Wafer iron*

30. *Waffle iron*

Teakettle. A special fireplace version had a tilter attached to its cast iron base allowing the cook to pour hot water right from the crane, so she wouldn't have to lift the heavy pot. Cast iron teakettles usually had short legs, handy when placing them over the coals or simply resting them on the hearth. More usual models, similar to those in use today, were also available in the old days. They were frequently made of brass or copper. (23)

Tin kitchen. Also called a reflector oven, it was a cylindrical tin box, open on one side, which sat in front of the fire. Its shiny surfaces reflected the fire's heat onto the sides of the food not directly facing the fire. A clever device, it came in two versions. The simpler version was for baking and had a shelf intersecting its center for placing pies, muffins, and breads to bake. A more complicated version of the tin kitchen, for roasting, came equipped with a spit instead of a shelf. In addition to the spit, it had a spout for pouring off drippings as they accumulated, and a door in the back reflecting panel so the cook could check the progress of her roast without disturbing its position on the hearth. (24)

Toaster. Fireplace toasters came in many models. The earliest and simplest of which was a stationary wrought iron frame on three legs with a short handle. It (like the other toasters) was placed before the fire to toast its contents. "Improved" toasters featured a frame that rotated so the bread did not have to be removed to turn its other side to the fire. And in even later versions, the toaster handle was lengthened and hinged to the toast holder, so that with just a flick of the cook's wrist she could swivel the toast and expose its uncooked side to the fire. (25)

Trammel. An adjustable pothook that was used to hang cooking pots over the fire at different heights from the lugpole or crane. Common varieties were the sawtooth, chain-and-hook, and the hole-and-peg combinations. The cook could adjust and lock the trammel into different lengths, thereby changing the hanging pot's distance from the fire, and controlling the temperature of the cooking food. (26)

Trivet. A stand for supporting a footless cooking vessel, such as a frying pan, over the coals. They came in many designs, including round, and heart-shaped. Some had handles, others didn't. (27)

Toasting fork. A large, long-handled, two-tined fork with two small legs. It supported a tidbit of meat or bread to be cooked or toasted before the fire. The ends of the fork tines were often curved upwards so that the food would not fall off. (28)

Wafer iron. A long-handled, hinged iron for making wafers, a thin crisp cookie, at the fireplace. The wafer iron was the predecessor of the waffle iron. (29)

Waffle iron. A long-handled, hinged iron for making waffles in the fireplace. (30)

The Modern Fireplace and its Accessories for the Contemporary Open-Hearth Cook

In spite of the long list of early American cooking pots and implements just surveyed, to cook a meal in most any fireplace one needs surprisingly few accessories. Many of the implements, pots, and other materials you will need may already be on hand in your kitchen, on your workbench, or at your barbecue grill. A fireplace is, of course, a must, and although few of us will have a traditional cooking fireplace with its spacious hearth in our kitchens—or anywhere else in our homes, for that matter—this needn't be a drawback. Practically all of the cooking techniques described in this book can be executed in most any fireplace. The setting, or the furniture, rugs, and decorations that surround your fireplace, may be inhibiting factors for cooking. But fine carpeting, highly finished wood flooring, or a valuable area rug can be protected from spattering grease, straying embers, and other cooking mess, by temporarily covering them with a wool throw rug or carpet remnant for safety. The use of certain cooking implements will also help circumvent possible damage of this nature. Especially desirable for use in a pristine environment are tin kitchens, both for baking and roasting, since to use them one just pops the kitchen in front of a well-established fire. Other cooking implements and techniques that produce a minimum amount of mess and moving around of coals are described in the individual discussions of each implement's use in the technique chapters of this book.

The size of your fireplace will also be a major factor in determining how many foods one can cook in it simultaneously. Be realistic: a small fireplace may permit the preparation of only one dish at a time. This will be especially true if the hearth area is small and does not extend out into the room. A crane or a large trammel will increase the cooking capacity of a small fireplace, as a pot or two can be hung from it over the fire, while others are sitting over the coals or before the fire. So, if you intend to immerse yourself in fireplace cooking, you may want to investigate installing a crane or other pot-holders in your fireplace. Chapter 10, "Sources for Hearth Cookware and Accessories," lists craftsmen and other outlets that can provide a crane to fit most any fireplace opening.

Besides a fireplace, and basic cooking implements, a cook will need a few fireplace tools to manipulate burning logs and coals. A shovel and a pair of wood tongs will suffice for these tasks. Bellows are nice to have, too, but not absolutely necessary. A folded magazine or newspaper will do nicely in their place for fanning the fire.

After these basics for fire-building and –tending, you will need a few implements for cooking your meal. Happily, this needn't be a long list of expensive antiques. With a few items, probably most of which are already around the house, you can cook a delicious dinner in a fireplace. Here is a list of the bare necessities needed, today, for performing the basic cooking techniques at a hearth without a crane. Precisely how they, and the antiques inventoried earlier, are used is discussed in detail in the following chapters.

A First Inventory and Its Uses for the Contemporary Fireplace Cook

- Butcher's twine or other stout, natural cord
- Camp Dutch oven fitted with an interior rack (a circular wire baking rack for cooling cookies and cake layers)
- Dripping pan (any kitchen roasting pan or disposable foil baking or lasagna pan that is large enough and deep enough)
- Fire bricks, or a sturdy metal trivet with 1 to 2 inch-long legs
- Grill from a barbecue (round, square, or even hinged variety)
- Kitchen pots and pans and lids of various sizes.
- Meat thermometer
- Metal spatulas, spoons, forks, and tongs (barbecue or large kitchen cooking ones)
- Dozen new common nails, aluminum or steel, at least 1 inch long, of medium thickness, with or without heads
- Plank of clean, hard wood
- Pot-holders or barbecue mitts
- Reflecting panels made out of disposable oven liners.

For roasting. Butcher's twine for trussing a roast or fowl and hanging it in front of the fire to cook; reflecting panels, improvised from two disposable oven liners, screwed or wired together to form a free-standing V, and a large roasting, or other generous-sized pan underneath to catch the drippings. These will complete the implements needed to roast a delicious entrée. For roasting a fish, a plank of wood, aluminum foil, nails, and butcher's twine are all that is required.

For toasting. A large kitchen fork.

For broiling. Aluminum foil to cover the hearth cooking area and a barbecue grill supported over the coals on two fire bricks.

For boiling, simmering, stewing, etc. A suitably sized kitchen pot with a lid adapted to fireplace use by placing it on a grill supported by two firebricks or a trivet to raise it above the coals. Kettle lids were sometimes made of

17

copper, but were more commonly round slabs of wood with a hole in the center for removing with a lid lifter.

For baking. A cast iron Dutch oven with feet, a concave lid, and a rack placed in its bottom is a must. The rack could either be a cake rack, if your oven is large enough to accommodate one, or a wire Christmas wreath form. The oven is the only item on this beginner's list of cooking tools that will cost more than a few dollars and that may involve some leg work to obtain. Dutch ovens are always available from the Boy Scouts and a number of other sources listed in Chapter 10. We should add that they are well worth the price and effort to obtain, since they are not only the best all-around implement for fireplace baking, but can be used for frying, stewing, simmering, and other cooking techniques at the hearth, as well.

For frying and sautéing. A kitchen griddle or frying pan adapted to fireplace use by placing it on a grill supported by two firebricks or a trivet.

For browning off. Tongs for passing live coals over food to brown tops.

Naturally, as you become more skilled at fireplace cooking and your appetite is whetted for more elaborate meals, you will probably want a fuller complement of fireplace cooking tools and implements. Sources for reproductions of the original antiques are listed in Chapter 10, along with suggestions on how to go about collecting the authentic antiques. But, before you begin collecting, keep in mind the spirit of improvisation ever-present in the early American household. Don't be reluctant to bring your Chinese wok or fish poacher to the hearth, for, with a trivet or fire bricks for support, they will be equally as comfortable and useful here as in your modern kitchen.

Care of Fireplace Pots and Implements

Before we turn to our discussions of the actual performance of the basic cooking techniques at the hearth, here is how to clean and care for your fireplace cooking pots—especially the iron ones.

For ordinary kitchen pots and pans adapted for fireplace cooking, the general rule is to clean and care for them as you normally would. Rubbing a bar of soap on pots' exterior surfaces before using them at the fireplace will keep them from becoming overly blackened from the carbon of the fire, and will save you a lot of extra scrubbing at clean-up time. (Iron pots, of course, will hide this discoloration.)

New iron cooking pots as well as antique ones (as soon as their rust, paint, and other residual dirt have been removed), are both "cured" and cared for in the same way. Before cooking in a new iron pot, or a professionally cleaned antique one, you must season, or "cure" it first. To do this, first scrub the pot out well with detergent and hot water, rinse thoroughly, and dry. Next, apply a coating of vegetable oil, shortening, or spray shortening, to the interior surfaces (don't forget the underside of the lid). Then heat the pot in your modern oven until the grease begins to smoke. Be sure not to let the grease burn. Remove the pot and let it cool. It is now ready for cooking. (Another way to season cast iron pots, especially the Dutch oven, is to deep-fat fry foods in them the first few times they are used.) After your cooking is completed, clean your pot, but don't overdo this step. Often, wiping it out with a damp cloth is sufficient. Never use a scouring pad on seasoned cast iron. Dry pots well. Letting the warmth of the fire accomplish this for you is an easy way. Before you put the pot away, be sure to lightly regrease it, as a buildup of these layers of grease will "sweeten" the iron and protect it from rusting, avoid discoloration, and help prevent food from sticking. Your pot is now ready for the next cooking session. It will only have to be reseasoned if you boil liquids in it, or if an unknowing helper scrubs it out too well at the conclusion of a meal.

For long-term storage of cast iron, an application of Pam, a commercial non-stick, spray shortening for cooking surfaces, is recommended. Pam does not become sticky or gummy with age or become rancid as time passes, as will some other common vegetable oils, lards, and natural greases.

2

The Cooking Fire

Selecting Cooking Wood

Not just any wood will suffice for building a cooking fire. And while fruit crates, old lumber, and virtually any wooden scrap material will burn, certain firewood fuels are much more desirable than others and will allow the chef to accomplish his or her cooking tasks at the hearth with the greatest degree of ease, success, and safety.

The two essential properties of the best cooking woods are that they generate an even, intense heat and that they produce a good supply of red-hot coals as combustion proceeds. The wood of trees that fall under the general classification of "hardwoods" best satisfy these two criteria.

To fully understand why the hardwoods make the best cooking fuels, we should know how the heat of the fire is used in fireplace cooking to execute the basic techniques of baking, boiling, roasting, and frying.

Early American cooks, who prepared all of their food in the fireplace (and a splendid array at that, from dainty almond cakes to roast suckling pig), usually built one central fire on their cooking hearths. From this single source, all the energy for their various cooking activities was generated. A description of these fires from the period said that they were, at their best, small, clear, and brisk. Leaping flames, or a blaze filling the entire expanse of the hearth, dramatic as these displays might have been, were of little use to the fireplace cooks of yesterday. In front of a small, controllable fire, these cooks roasted and toasted food. Suspended from a crane or trammels above the fire, their soups, puddings, and one-pot meals boiled, simmered, steamed, and stewed. And to utilize still further the fire's energy, its coals were raked or scooped up and placed on the lids and underneath specially designed fireplace pots and implements to provide the heat necessary to bake, fry, and broil simultaneously on other areas of the hearth.

From this brief glimpse of the basic fireplace cooking techniques, one can quickly see that the fire's flame rarely made contact with the food in this tradition of cooking. The most valuable qualities of the fire were that it produced a ready and plentiful supply of hot coals for performing certain cooking methods, and gave a manageable blaze for the others.

Although the special wood (hardwood) needed for a cooking fire may cost a little more and may take somewhat more trouble to locate, it's worth it! We can't emphasize strongly enough how frustrating it will be to try to duplicate the cooking techniques described in this book with wood that burns too rapidly, smokes, pops, or, what is most important, produces a few or no coals.

Wood falls into two general categories: hard and soft, with the logs of hardwood trees, as we have mentioned earlier, the preferred variety for cooking. While hardwoods are more difficult to ignite, burn less vigorously, and have a shorter flame than do the softwoods, the fires they produce are hotter, last longer, and generate more coals.

Some of the hardwoods we recommend for cooking are: ash, apple, cherry, hickory, black locust, sugar maple, and red oak. Here are a few of the special characteristics of these woods.

Ash is considered by some to be the most desirable of the hardwoods. It can be burned in a green, or unseasoned, state, as the anonymous author of the poem "Which Wood Burns Best" noted in his praise of this wood:

> But ash wood wet and ash wood dry,
> A king shall warm his slippers by.

Oak, another favored hardwood, gives off a uniform heat and short flames. It also produces a good, steady supply of glowing coals.

The wood of fruit and nut trees is among the most highly prized of the hardwoods. These woods impart a flavor and fragrance to food they cook that resembles their fruits and nuts. The smoke will also lend an aroma that will perfume your fireplace kitchen and cooking area.

By comparison, the softwoods—pine, spruce, fir, and willow, for example—are easier to ignite than hardwoods because of their high resin content. Like hardwoods, they also produce a very hot fire. But this is where their advantages for cooking end. Fires built of softwood have the tendency to pop, sending dangerous sparks and embers flying out of the hearth area, potentially harming the cook and burning the rug. These woods burn very rapidly, requiring almost constant attention in order to maintain a steady cooking temperature. Their fires generate too meager a supply of coals to permit such techniques as

21

baking, grilling, and frying. And their resinous quality can impart a peculiar smell and taste to your food.

The only role that softwoods seem to perform successfully in the cooking fire is as an aid in fire-starting. Although we've never found it necessary, some

The Relative Ratings of a Variety of Dried Hardwoods*

	Ash Red oak White oak Beech Birch Aspen Hickory Basswood Hard maple Pecan Dogwood	Soft maple Cherry Walnut	Elm Sycamore Gum	Cottonwood Yellow poplar
Relative amount of heat	High	Medium	Medium	Low
Easy to burn	Yes	Yes	Medium	Yes
Easy to split	Yes	Yes	No	Yes
Does it have heavy smoke?	No	No	Medium	Medium
Does it pop or throw sparks?	No	No	No	No
General rating and remarks	Excellent	Good	Fair (*contains too much water when green*)	Fair (*but good for kindling*)

*Chart excerpted from Leaflet No. 559 U.S. Department of Agriculture, Forest Service: Firewood for Your Fireplace: Selection, Purchase, Use.

authorities suggest that a log or two of softwood mixed in with the hardwoods will make your fire easier to ignite.

The chart in this chapter covers the relative ease of starting, splitting, and other characteristics of specific woods.

Buying Firewood

There are two options available for obtaining firewood: cutting and gathering it yourself in the woods, or paying someone else to do this for you. Buying your wood is obviously the easier—and the more expensive—alternative; and if your time is at a premium or if your skills and muscular abilities are unequal to the task of felling trees, it's also the most sensible. And don't forget the sawing, splitting, and hauling that the transformation of standing timber to ready-to-use firewood entails.

We prefer to buy our cooking wood. If you live in a fairly rural area, as we do, the purchasing process will usually only involve checking the classified ads in your local newspaper for the most competitive price. If you live in the city, you may have to look a little harder and drive a little farther to find competitive prices for firewood. However, price is not the sole factor to consider when choosing a wood supplier. Here are some guidelines for getting the best value out of your wood purchase.

Firewood is normally sold by the standard cord or fraction of a cord. This measurement should not be confused with either a "face cord" (sometimes called a short cord), which measures eight-by-four-by-one (or two) feet, or a long cord, which measures eight-by-four-by-four plus feet. The standard cord stack is eight feet long, four feet wide, and four feet high, and contains a total of 128 cubic feet.

Because the standard cord is a volume measurement, the amount of solid wood in a cord can vary greatly, depending on whether the wood pieces are straight or crooked, round or split, and large or small in diameter. These variations in shape and size can affect considerably the actual amount of wood you receive, and can account for a range of up to fifty cubic feet of wood in the supposedly standard cord. As a rule, round wood in large diameters, or split wood, neatly stacked, yields the most solid wood per cord.

Firewood is also sold by the truckload. Here, the amount of wood in a load can be estimated by the type and size of the delivery vehicle. The average pickup truck holds about two standard face cords—this is equivalent to only about 25 to 50 percent of the amount of wood in a standard cord. By comparison, a dump truck can hold up to four standard cords. And a large pulpwood truck with a wood rack holds anywhere from six to nine standard cords.

Another way wood is sold is by weight. If you buy wood by weight, be warned against purchasing water (which is very heavy) instead of wood. Look for the driest wood possible! Not only will you be getting more wood for your money, but you won't have to wait six to ten months while it seasons before you can burn it. Although green or unseasoned wood burns, it does so only with a lot of coaxing. It is harder to ignite than dry wood, produces less heat, and is more apt to form dangerous creosote and soot deposits in your chimney. Cracks in the ends of the logs are an indication the wood is dry or seasoned.

Here are some other factors that can affect the price of firewood.

Fruit and nut woods, because of their attractive fragrance, are in great demand, a demand that has made them the most expensive of the hardwoods. But keep in mind that they don't produce as much heat as some of the other less costly varieties, and, in practice, only a log or two of these species need be added to a fire built of the less expensive hardwoods to produce enough flavor and fragrance for entire cooking sessions.

Seasoned wood costs more per cord than green wood. So, you can save yourself some money if you have a little foresight about your firewood needs. A well-ventilated, sheltered area, out-of-doors, is all you need to store your green wood. In general, wood cut in the fall or winter of one year is seasoned and ready for use by the fall of next year.

Where you live also affects the price of wood. Obviously, firewood is bound to be dearer in New York City than it is in a lumber town in Oregon, so, for city dwellers, a trip to the nearby countryside with your station wagon may be worthwhile.

Picking up, splitting, stacking, and unloading your own wood saves time and labor for the firewood dealer and can translate into dollar savings for you, as well.

The time of year when you buy your wood also affects its price. In summer, prices are usually lower than in fall and winter, when the demand for firewood increases. Miss Beecher, author of *Domestic Receipt Book, 1846,* advised the thrifty American homemaker: "Buy your wood in August or September, when it is cheapest and plenty."

Cutting Your Own

There is an old saying about wood. It warms you twice. Once when you cut it, and again when you burn it. And, with the price of firewood as high as it is and continuing to rise with the increasing popularity of woodstoves, cutting your own wood can be an attractive alternative. While it is hard, hot work, time-consuming, and frequently dangerous for the novice, it is undoubtedly the cheapest way of obtaining good cooking wood.

Here are some ideas about where to find trees for cutting for the would-be Paul Bunyan. If you are fortunate enough to own a woodlot, proper culling or thinning of your timber will not only provide you with firewood, but will improve the quality and rate of growth of your remaining trees. If you don't own a woodlot, it is often possible for a nominal fee to buy cutting and salvage rights on municipal, state, or federal lands.

Another, even easier source of firewood for the do-it-yourselfer is the local dump. Many towns prohibit open burning, and as much as 30 percent of the debris discarded in these areas may be usable wood fiber—the logs, limbs, and tops of trees toppled by storms or cleared in real estate development. This wood is often, but not always, free for the taking.

If cutting your own wood interests you, more specific information on woodlot management and splitting, seasoning, and storing firewood can be obtained from the conservation departments of most states or from your local County Extension Service agents.

Building the Cooking Fire

Building or laying a fire may on the surface appear easy, but there is a real art and even some tradition involved in constructing a fire suitable for cooking.

Historically, ways of laying a cooking fire differed in various areas of developing America. In New England, for example, the common practice was to build this fire on andirons that were modified especially for cooking These andirons looked very much like any in use today, except for a series of hooks that protruded from their vertical columns to support the spitted meat, fish, and fowl as it roasted before the fire.

Although cooking, or spit, andirons were popular in the North, in some of the more central colonies—Berks County, Pennsylvania, specifically—the ancestry of the settlers favored a tradition of building cooking fires directly on the hearth floor. We recommend this method and describe a variation on it next. Its distinct advantage is that it requires no special or expensive equipment. While antique cooking andirons are helpful for open-hearth cooking and do add an authentic air to your fireplace, they are very rare and costly. And reproductions won't be much cheaper, since a skilled blacksmith will have to be commissioned to make them.

Here is a simple way of stacking wood for a cooking fire that the authors have found most successful, and that requires, for starters, only six good-sized pieces of split and seasoned hardwood, kindling, newspaper, matches, and a clean, clear hearth.

To lay your fire, begin by placing two of the logs on the hearth floor with their ends at right angles to, and almost touching, the rear wall of your fireplace. These first two logs will act as supports or "andirons" for the remaining logs. Next, lay the remaining four logs across the top of the bottom two, parallel to the back wall of the fireplace, and leave some space between them for the fire to breathe. Kindling (sticks, crumpled paper, pine cones, wood shavings, etc.) should then be placed on top of the logs and stuffed into the cracks between them and into the low tunnel formed by the stacking configuration.

Ignite the kindling, with a makeshift torch of twisted newspaper. Next, hold the torch up the open chimney flue to encourage a healthy draft. The fire can also be fanned at this point with a bellows, magazine, or folded newspaper to ensure a strong start.

Stacking your wood in this manner leaves a natural space for the coals to accumulate in, and gives the cook easy access to them as they are needed for baking, frying, and broiling, without having to disturb the fire's design.

It is most important to maintain the fire's basic configuration when adding new logs and until all of your cooking is completed. About two hours and two generous armfuls of firewood are needed to prepare the average full-course meal. From our experience, the upper logs burn with greater vigor than do the andiron logs. They will need to be replenished sooner and more frequently, but this is an easy task requiring only the careful placement of a fresh log or two on the andiron logs.

The andiron logs will not need to be replaced as often, but, when they do,

How to stack a double cooking fire.

substantial rebuilding and manipulation of the fire's hot logs may be necessary in order to maintain the cooking fire's basic shape. Using green or unseasoned wood for the andiron legs can delay and even eliminate this last step, especially when preparing foods that cook quickly.

For roasting a large piece of meat such as a suckling pig, or for cooking numerous smaller items simultaneously, like ducks, chickens, or Cornish hens, it will be necessary to build a wider or double version of the basic cooking fire. If your fireplace is big enough to accommodate cooking on this scale, a double cooking fire should be adequate for the most ambitious of meals. To build a fire of this design, use three andiron supports, instead of two, and proceed in the same way outline earlier, with top logs, kindling, etc.

As a general rule, the length of the fire should equal the length of the spitted food in order for the food to roast evenly. And, while this double contiguous fire can be extended further with the addition of more andiron logs, we have rarely found it necessary, nor have we found many fireplaces large enough to contain a fire of this size.

Another important guideline to remember when building a cooking fire is that its size should be governed by the standard length (about eighteen inches) of most pieces of split and cut firewood, and not necessarily by the size of one's fireplace. For example, in a large early American cooking hearth the basic cooking fire, stacked as outlined earlier, measures eighteen inches square. It will appear dwarfed by the enormous proportions of most early fireplaces, but this is fine. The best cooking fires do not fill up the entire hearth area, but leave plenty of free space, so cooking over coals raked apart from the central fire can proceed with ease. If you are fortunate enough to have such an exceptionally spacious hearth, you also might build two of these fires and use one for roasting and the other for your other cooking activities. This was a common practice of the early American housewife and is analogous today to our turning on our oven and cooktop simultaneously.

In the generally smaller modern fireplaces where hearth area is at a premium, the length of the logs used to stack the fire is even more critical. Don't fill up the entire hearth space in your contemporary fireplace with your fire, unless it is absolutely necessary, as doing so will severely limit your cooking possibilities. Should your fireplace be very small, it may be necessary to have your logs cut shorter than the eighteen-inch standard so that the fire does not extend into the room when it has been stacked according to the authors' instructions.

Here is a description of the lengths to which our ancestors went to build fires for preparing their meals and heating their homes. A North American writer is describing his home in New England at the end of the eighteenth century.

...the fuel was supplied by our own woods–sweet-scented hickory, snapping chestnut, odoriferous oak, and reeking, fizzling ash–the hot juice of the latter being a sovereign antidote for the ear ache. These were laid in huge piles, all alive with sap, on the tall, gaunt andirons... The building of the fire was a real architectural achievement, favoured by the wide yawning fireplace, and was always begun by daybreak. There was first a back-log, from fifteen to four and twenty inches in diameter and five feet long, imbedded in the ashes; then came a top-log, then a fore-stick, then a middle-stick and then a heap of kindlings, reaching from the bowels down to the bottom. A-top of all was a pyramid of smaller fragments, artfully adjusted, with spaces for the blaze... Friction matches had not then been sent from the regions of brimstone, to enable every boy or beggar to carry a conflagration in his pocket. If there were no coals left from last night's fire and none to be borrowed from the neighbors, resort was had to flint, steel, and tinder-box. Often when the fire was dull, and the steel soft and the tinder damp, the striking of fire was a task requiring both energy and patience.*

Another early American fire-building tradition is mentioned in this account–the back-log. The back-log was the name given to the huge green logs that were placed along the rear walls of the kitchen hearth. Some of these logs could better be described as whole small trees, and were reportedly of such immense proportions that they had to be hauled into the kitchen by a team of horses. The back-log served two purposes. It protected the back wall of the fireplace from the deterioration that was caused by the intense heat of the constant cooking fires. And, banked with ashes, it safely held smoldering coals overnight, in readiness for lighting the morning fire. In the South, the traditional Yule Log was originally a back-log. The custom arose for the large plantation owners to grant a holiday from chores to their slaves as long as the back-log continued to burn during the Christmas season. Naturally the greener and the bigger a log that could be found, the better. Some of these first Yule logs were said to have lasted for a good week or more.

Regulating the Heat of the Cooking Fire

Today, because we are accustomed to simply turning a dial or pushing a button to achieve a desired oven temperature, it may seem intimidating at first to try to use the comparatively inexact science of cooking with a fire. But we are

---

*Molly Harrison, The Kitchen in History (New York: Charles Scribner's Sons, 1972), p. 99.

confident that you can learn to control the fire and to judge its heat with only a little practice and the application of some common sense. Here are some general remarks on this topic to help you avoid burning or undercooking your fireplace dinners. (More detailed information on regulating the cooking heat for specific implements, the tin kitchen, Dutch oven, etc. is given in the practical sections of the technique chapters.)

Regulating the heat of a cooking fire is a two-step process that involves building and maintaining a constant and hot enough fire, then exposing the food to the right amount of heat so that it cooks at a desirable rate.

Maintaining a constant and hot enough fire is the cook's first job and her greatest single control A fire laid on the hearth in the method outlined earlier in this chapter will generate enough coals approximately one hour after it is ignited for Dutch oven baking, spider frying, or gridiron broiling. Reflector oven roasting, and baking, toasting, and boiling, techniques that rely on the direct and reflected heat of the central fire, can be started somewhat earlier. The cook, then, has only to remember to replenish the fire with additional wood as needed until the cooking is completed.

Once a constant and hot enough fire is reached and maintained and a supply of glowing coals has accumulated, the next step is to judge the amount of coals needed and the best distance from the fire for cooking your food.

For fireplace cooking, and for cooking in general, we have observed that a chef needs only three basic temperatures—low, medium, and high—to prepare practically all foods and recipes successfully. In most cases, variations in temperature of anywhere from 50 to 100 degrees seem to have very little effect on the quality of the finished product, as our experiences with the unreliable thermostat of our supposedly exact electric and gas ovens have proven. And while oven and cooking thermometers can determine the intensity of the fireplace environment and the internal temperature of the cooking food, we have never found such precise measurements necessary. And neither did the original fireplace cooks, who, of course, didn't have such gadgets available to them.

In reality, cooks today are still relying on these same broad heat classifications. On most modern cooktops, the controls are usually marked with only Low, Medium, and High, and we all proceed without hesitation and with little or no difficulty, with only these general guides to follow. Added to this is the irony that, in this era of high technology, professional and gourmet household cooks prefer gas ranges over their electric counterparts, even though they acknowledge that more precise adjustments in temperatures are possible with electrical appliances, especially in the lower temperatures, than the gas appliances. Most cooks account for their bias by saying that the flame produced by the gas helps them judge the fire's heat with greater accuracy. Which brings us to the most reliable ways of gauging the heat on your dial-less cooking hearth.

The best way to determine the fire's intensity is for the cook to use her own senses of sight and touch. As primitive as this may sound, we have found that most cooks have opened their modern ovens enough times—to baste roasting chickens, turn broiling meat, or test a baking cake—to recognize the commonly used oven temperatures by feel. This is invaluable experience in open-hearth cooking, where the cook's skin is constantly exposed to the fire and can serve as a natural thermometer.

Skin sensitivity—combined with the cook's frequent observation of whether the meat or pie crust is browning too quickly or the soup is boiling rather than simmering—should provide sufficient information to allow the cook to select the best distance from the fire for the food or to alter the amount of coals needed to achieve the proper cooking temperature.

Adjustments for raising or lowering the cooking heat when roasting, toasting, and reflector oven baking (techniques that rely on the direct and reflected heat of the fire) can obviously be made by moving the food either closer to or farther away from the fire. When these techniques are being accomplished with implements that rest on the hearth floor, a push towards or away from the central fire will suffice. On the crane, S hooks or trammels enable the fireplace cook to make temperature corrections by raising or lowering the pots of cooking food.

When cooking with coals, adjusting the heat is simply a matter of the quantity of coals used. The fewer the coals under the pots and on their lids, the slower the cooking action; more coals will make for quicker cooking.

While these methods of temperature measurement may seem imprecise, they do work surprisingly well. As Eliza Leslie, the nineteenth-century fireplace cook and author, demonstrated by the inclusion of a soufflé recipe—to be prepared in a Dutch oven, no less—in her famous and highly regarded cookbook. A soufflé is surely one of the more delicate and temperature-sensitive dishes, and a challenge to prepare even with the most sophisticated and predictable sources of cooking heat.

A last observation on coping with the heat of a cooking fire: it takes slightly longer for foods to cook in the fireplace than in a modern appliance. While this may lead to undercooking, fortunately, from our observation, the fireplace cook who does not have exact temperature controls as a guide is naturally more inclined to proceed cautiously. After all, one can always speed up the cooking process by raising the heat, but once the top of the cake is burned, there's no retrieving it!

Safety Precautions at the Hearth

A discussion of the cooking fire would be incomplete without a few words on how to work with it safely.

Although early American women cooked with long-handled pots and utensils, being burned and even burning one's house down were frequent misfortunes, especially in the Colonial period when fireplaces and chimneys were rudely constructed. As a safety measure, these women kept their long, heavy woolen cloaks close at hand to smother any flames in the event they were faced with such an emergency. They were also extremely careful when handling live coals and hot fats. The floor near their cooking hearths was swept constantly, and the hearth itself scrubbed often to keep it free from grease. The twenty-first-century cook should emulate these safety measures. Here are some additional precautions for fireplace cooks today.

Make sure your chimney has been checked and cleaned recently for creosote build-up, a common cause of chimney fires and a result of burning green wood and softwoods.

Don't use woods that spark or pop for cooking purposes. In this category are the softwoods: cedar, juniper, hemlock, spruce, etc., discussed earlier in this chapter.

Don't use charcoal or synthetic or newspaper logs to cook food. While charcoal can be used safely outdoors, indoors, where toxic fumes can collect, its use can be dangerous. Synthetic or newspaper logs won't produce high enough cooking temperatures or an adequate supply of coals, and may have harmful chemical additives. Avoid lighter fluid or commercial fire starters, too. They can impart a funny taste to your food.

Don't allow roasting or broiling food to drip directly on the hearth. Always use a dripping pan, or improvise one from several thicknesses of aluminum foil, to catch these juices and fats. An accumulation of grease on the hearth will not only create a dreadful mess, but can cause a serious fire, as well.

Don't wear loose clothing that can dangle over or near the flames and catch fire when you are cooking. Sturdy, comfortable shoes are also in order to protect toes from hot embers.

Store ashes in a non-combustible container. (By the way, cold ashes are beneficial fertilizer for your flower and vegetable gardens.)

Keep a fire extinguisher handy, and know how to use it!

3

Baking

Of the many fireplace cooking techniques discussed in this book, baking on an open hearth is perhaps the most foreign to our modern imaginations. Unless one is an ardent camper, baking a pie or cake with a wood fire has an almost magical quality about it. It never fails to amaze our dinner guests that everything turns out done to perfection–the breads rise, the cakes are tender and light, and the pie crusts evenly browned. And these accomplishments are all achieved without the use of a thermostatically controlled oven, and in spite of our seemingly casual attitude about baking times. In order to help you understand how to duplicate these results yourself, here is a description of what early Americans baked in their fireplaces and how they did it.

In Early America

Baking, or the use of enclosed heat to cook food, on the first American hearths was a very uncomplicated process, and the resulting cakes and breads reflected this. They were a far cry from what we are accustomed to eating today. Corn bread, johnny- or journey cakes, ash cakes, hoecakes, rye n'Injun, and scratch backs were some of the unfamiliar but amusing-sounding baked foods consumed in the Colonies. Many of the names aptly describe the distinctive characteristics of these baked goods, and their method of preparation, as well.

Johnnycakes were "good keepers," staying fresh for a number of days. For this reason they became a saddlebag staple and were also called journeycakes by some. Ash cakes were baked, as their name implies, in a wrapping of leaves amidst the hot fireplace coals. Hoecakes were so-called because they were baked on the end of a broad iron hoe or shovel, often over an open fire in the field on a hungry farmer's lunch break. And the rough crust of scratch backs were notorious for scratching the roof of the diner's mouth.

Uniquely American, these breads and cakes were nothing like the delicate, light-textured, perfectly browned, and mild-tasting items we find on our super-market shelves and in our bakeries today. Frequently just a mixture of corn-meal, grease, water, and salt shaped into small cakes with one's hands, these baked goods were dense from a lack of leavening, strongly flavored from the commonly used molasses sweetener, and often charred by the fire.

How were these early breads and cakes received by the palate of the popu-lation? In the 1700s, visiting Englishmen wrote to their relatives that they found them extremely harsh and unpleasant and thought such fare was fit only for slaves. In another period account, a more gracious or perhaps better-fed guest, recorded that he had enjoyed the simple hoecake. But regardless of how they tasted, that these cakes were even edible was a tribute to the Colonial housewife's imagination and ingenuity, and to the cuisine of the American Indian, from which many of her recipes were in part derived.

To appreciate fully these breads and cakes, one has to take into account that our first cooks were severely limited by a scarcity of ingredients. Wheat flour, sugar, butter, milk, eggs, and spices—the elementary materials of baking today—were in short supply then, and were often too expensive for daily use when available.

Compounding the problem of the bare larder was the shortage of brick bake ovens, the most sophisticated baking implement of the period. While some villages shared a communal bake oven, more isolated settlers did not enjoy the benefit of such a luxury until the brick-making trade became more firmly estab-lished in this country. Also lacking in household kitchens were scales, stan-dardized leavening agents, and measuring spoons and cups.

Pearlash, the first leavening agent (known now as baking powder), even though discovered in the mid-eighteenth century by an American, was regard-ed with great suspicion at first. Many cooks felt its inclusion in a recipe was harmful to one's health and ruined the flavor of baked goods. Pearlash was originally derived from leaching firewood ashes, so these concerns about its purity and healthfulness may have been well founded.

After the Revolutionary War, when the men were back tending the farms and trade with other nations resumed, the country's economy in general improved, too, and with it, the quality and diversity of baked foods. Fireplace baking from this point on reached culinary heights remarkable even by today's standards. It was not uncommon for cookbooks of this era to include recipes for French bread, lady fingers, sponge cake, and puff pastry, or for a variety of such delicacies to grace the tables of wealthy landowners. Sophisticated baking was especially found in the South, which was known for its lavish hospitality and where slaves did the time-consuming and hot work required to prepare beaten biscuits and other specialties at the hearth and in the bake oven.

Among the first baking techniques American women used in their fireplaces was one copied from the native Indian squaws. This technique involved simply sweeping a spot clean on the hearth and placing the unbaked bread or cake, wrapped in corn husks or cabbage leaves, directly on the heated hearth stones or in the fire's coals to cook. A primitive method of baking by any civilization's standards, the resulting baked goods were frequently charred by fire and coated with ashes.

A refinement of this procedure was to place an inverted iron or crockery pot (sometimes the bottom of the Dutch oven) over the dough. Hot coals were then placed around and heaped on top of this inverted pot to form a crude oven. A makeshift arrangement, this method of baking worked adequately and can successfully be copied in your fireplace today. It can be observed in practice at the re-creation of the 1627 Pilgrim settlement, Plimoth Plantation in Plymouth, Massachusetts.

Another method of baking that our first housewives employed was to bake their dough on a wooden board. The predecessor of our cookie sheet, this board (almost any piece of sturdy, clean, flat wood qualified) was propped up before the fire in order to cook a layer of dough or thick batter. Bannocks, a flat oatmeal cake of Scottish origin, were traditionally prepared in this manner. Hence the baking board came to be called a Bannock board by many. Other foods could be baked on these boards, as well. Eliza Leslie recommends this method of preparation in the following recipe for johnnycake from her *Directions for Cookery, In Its Various Branches:*

Johnny Cake

Sift a quart of Indian meal into a pan; make a hole in the middle, pour in a pint of warm water. Mix the meal and water gradually into a batter, adding a small teaspoon of salt. Beat it very hard, and for a long time, till it becomes quite light. Then spread it thick and even on a stout piece of smooth board. Place it upright on the hearth before a clear fire, with a flat iron or something of the sort to support the board behind, and bake it well. Cut it into squares, and split and butter them hot.

While the authors have not personally tested Miss Leslie's johnnycake recipe, we have tried to duplicate this baking technique. We must confess that we found it impossible to achieve satisfactory results by baking on a board, and can't recommend it with confidence to the modern cook. Our repeated efforts were plagued with uneven baking, and cookies that slowly slid down the board, no matter how slight its incline, onto the hearth before the baking was completed. Letting the cakes "set" or dry out first, by placing the board in a horizontal position before the fire, as was suggested in a twentieth-century article on the fireplace cooking, didn't solve this problem for us, either.

Among the most reliable devices developed for fireplace baking, devices which were widely used by everyday housewives of moderate means to accomplish this task, were the Dutch oven, reflector oven, and baking griddle. A description of these implements and their use is given in the practical section of this chapter, which follows. These utensils give reliable results, are simple to use, and, with the exception of the griddle, are relatively inexpensive, since reproductions of their antique models are currently being produced.

But before we turn to their use, and to baking today in your fireplace, we would like to describe the most advanced baking oven developed during the fireplace cooking era—the beehive oven.

Beehive ovens, as their name suggests, were large dome-or beehive-shaped brick compartments in which cakes, breads, and other foods whose flavors were enhanced by a steady, moderate heat, were baked. In the earliest fireplaces, as we have seen, beehive ovens were built behind the cooking hearth with their doors opening into the back wall of the fireplace at approximately waist level. In order to preheat, test, insert, or remove food from these ovens, the cook actually had to step onto, or at best lean over, the hearth, bringing her long, full skirts dangerously close to the ever-present central cooking fire.

In later fireplaces, this design was modified, and bake ovens were built to one side of the fireplace, so that their doors were now located on the wall next to the hearth, and they opened directly into the room. Here the cook didn't have to enter the hearth fire area when using the bake oven, a safer and more convenient arrangement.

These indoor bake ovens shared the central fireplace chimney flue as a means of draft. Their doors were at first just slabs of wood, pushed into place, which tightly fitted the mouths of the ovens. These were later replaced by non-flammable and more durable iron doors properly hinged to the oven opening. In hotter climates bake ovens were frequently separate structures built entirely outside the main house, with their own sheds to protect both them and the cooks on baking day from the elements.

Baking breads and cakes and other foods in the beehive oven produced, with practice and experience, delicious and predictable results, but it was an arduous and time-consuming task. Depending on the size of one's family, baking in this oven was undertaken only once or at the very most twice a week.

To bake in this oven, one had to first preheat or "fire" it. Firing the oven was literally what preheating entailed. A fire of special oven wood was built directly on the bake oven's brick floor. Oven wood was merely dry, hardwood cut into small pieces of equal length. The wood was often reserved expressly for bake oven fires. This fire was kept burning inside the oven until the oven had reached the desired baking temperature—a process which sometimes took up the greater part of the day. During the preheating period the fire was frequently replenished, stoked, and its coals re-distributed to produce even heating of the oven's bricks. While the oven was heating the cooks used the time to prepare the large quantities of pies, cakes, breads, and other foods to be baked in it later.

Oven temperature was determined by the "bare arm" method, or by "trying" the oven with a bit of flour. The bare arm technique is described in an early cookbook as follows:

> For pies, cakes, and white bread, the heat of the oven should be such that you can hold your hand and arm (in it) while you count to 40; for brown bread, meats, beans, Indian puddings, and pumpkin pies, it should be hotter, so that you can only hold it in while you count to 20.*

To "try" the oven with flour, the cook sprinkled a handful on its floor and noted the rate at which it browned. If the flour browned too quickly or burned, the oven was too hot, and if it browned too slowly, it was too cold.

Obviously, experience counted!

When the oven was deemed hot enough, the remains of the fire were removed with a long-handled ash shovel, and its floor was swept clean. Next, fresh leaves were spread on the oven's floor and a layer of cornmeal was dusted over them. Since most cooks did not own enough baking pans to accommodate all the baked goods the oven held at one firing, this prevented the unbaked bread dough, pies, and cakes from sticking to the oven's floor or scorching.

To cool slightly the hot roof of the oven, and to remove any lingering stray ashes that might drift down and stick to the surface of the baking foods, the upper part of the oven was quickly brushed with a wet broom. The steam created by its moisture also produced a lovely glazed crust on the baked goods.

Foods requiring the hottest temperatures were baked first. These generally included breads, cakes, and pies. When these were completed and removed, successive loads which needed more moderate heat were put into the oven and allowed to cook slowly, occasionally overnight. Among the foods in this

---

*Molly Harrison, The Kitchen In History (New York: Charles Scribner's Sons, 1972)

latter category were crocks of beans, casseroles, and pumpkin and Indian puddings. And even when the oven had become too cool for "cooking" food, its remaining warmth was sometimes utilized by the thrifty homemaker to dry her herbs.

While these brick ovens produced excellent results, we should add that they generally were to be found only in the more comfortable households—and, of course, in professional bakeries. But it was known practice for homemakers of more modest means to pay their local baker to bake their foods in his beehive oven for them.

Techniques for Today

Thus far we have described opposite ends of the spectrum concerning fireplace baking techniques. But, since the majority of us do not live in restorations with beehive bake ovens, and are not interested in reverting to a charred caveman cuisine, exemplified earlier by the ash cake and baking board, we have focused the practical section of this chapter on baking in your fireplace today using the methods of early American housewives.

The average woman of yesterday accomplished her daily baking (as did her more affluent neighbors who owned bake ovens, when they wished to prepare only a few items) with the Dutch oven, reflector oven, and hanging griddle. We will first describe the technique of baking in the Dutch oven, as it is a most versatile piece of equipment, almost foolproof to use, and does not require a fireplace crane to support it. Most important, of the three baking implements mentioned, the Dutch oven disperses heat most evenly on all surfaces of foods baked in it.

Before we delve into the specific use of the Dutch oven, here are some general observations on baking in your fireplace which are true for all three implements.

Don't worry too much about exact oven temperatures. We have intentionally omitted them from this book, and we feel they are particularly irrelevant for baking. Instead, we have indicated low, medium, and high heats for the recipes. If you are very hesitant about this informal approach, a portable oven thermometer could be placed inside the Dutch oven or on the shelf of the reflector oven until you become more experienced and comfortable with approximating correct fireplace baking temperatures. We have never used an oven thermometer for fireplace baking, however, and don't think you will find one necessary.

The placement of the Dutch oven, reflector oven, and hanging griddle in relation to the fire, and the amount of coals needed for baking as described in this chapter, have been determined for a moderate oven, about 325 to 350 degrees. If you are substituting one of your own recipes when trying out any of these techniques, you may have to adjust the heat accordingly, although we have found that most foods can be successfully baked using this one average temperature range.

Judgment and caution are especially important in fireplace baking. We recommend that you check your baking food frequently to be sure that it is progressing to your satisfaction. The greatest danger in baking, and one whose damages cannot be remedied, is for cooking to proceed too rapidly with too much heat, causing the outside of food to be done before the inside is thoroughly cooked.

In short, while most anything can be baked in the fireplace using Dutch oven, reflector oven, and hanging griddle, large cakes and the more delicate ones, such as angel food or chiffon, should probably be avoided, unless you are very experienced or courageous. Even Eliza Leslie cautioned her expert fireplace cooking audience:

> It is safest when practicable, to send all large cakes to a professional baker... It may be recommended to novices in the art of baking, to do everything in little time or in very shallow pans; there being then less risk than with a large thick cake.

The Dutch Oven

Dutch ovens, beehive ovens notwithstanding, were the best all-around baking devices of the fireplace cooking era. Unlike the ones sold today for use with modern cooktops and ovens, the original Dutch oven had three short legs, a lid with a raised edge, and usually a bail, another name for a handle. Although this version has long since disappeared from our kitchens, you may recall it from your scout or camping days, for it is still commonly used in campfire cooking.

Following is the basic technique for baking in the Dutch oven, which in the authors' estimation is still the foremost implement available for fireplace baking today.

One hour before you plan to begin baking in your Dutch oven, lay and ignite your fire as described in Chapter 2, The Cooking Fire. This will allow adequate time for the fire to produce the coals necessary to begin baking. Roughly two small shovelfuls, or enough coals to form a single layer under the oven and on its lid, are needed to achieve a temperature suitable for baking in the Dutch oven. Some more coals will be needed later to sustain its heat until the contents are done. When you have judged the fire to have produced these coals, it's time to preheat your oven.

To preheat the Dutch oven, pick a convenient spot on the hearth for the baking to take place, and shovel a small amount of hot coals here. A good location for baking is one that is easily accessible to the cook, but where she won't trip over the oven, and one that is not too close to the central fire. Place the oven, lid on, over these coals and shovel more coals onto its lid. Ten minutes later your oven will be sufficiently preheated and ready for baking.

The recipe mixture should then be poured into the appropriately sized and shaped pan and placed on a wire rack inside the Dutch oven. Sometimes, if the baking pan fits snugly inside the oven, to avoid spills or burned fingers, it may be easier to reverse this step, by placing the empty pan or pie shell and rack inside the oven first, and then pouring or placing your batter into its container. This suggestion is especially helpful for custard and pumpkin pie fillings, and the more liquid cake batters.

The wire rack mentioned is essential for successful Dutch oven baking. It permits air circulation beneath the food being baked, prevents scorching of the bottom of your pies, cakes, and breads, and avoids damage to your Pyrex and pottery pans, which may break on direct contact with the intense heat of the oven's iron bottom. It is also important to note here that Dutch ovens are not sold with this vital accessory.

Historically, in place of this wire rack, cooks tempered the heat of the Dutch oven's iron floor by covering its bottom with a layer of ashes or sand. And while we are sure that this worked well for them, our preference is a circular cake rack, the kind used for cooling cakes and cookies. Only the largest Dutch ovens will accommodate these racks, but the authors have used wire Christmas wreath forms with great success in smaller ovens. Campers frequently use bottle caps or crumpled foil on the bottoms of their Dutch ovens to create the same effect.

After the baking mixture is safely in the oven on its rack, replace the lid and replenish the coals, top and bottom, placing slightly more coals on the lid or underneath to distribute the oven's heat appropriately for the food to be baked. The chart at the end of this section details the proportionate amount of coals for baking most recipes.

Be very careful not to burn yourself when maneuvering the hot, heavy lid of the Dutch oven. Use a very thick potholder, or, even better, an asbestos barbecue mitt, to protect your hands. A bale hook with a wooden handle is also handy for this task. Such hooks can often be bought inexpensively at flea markets from dealers who specialize in antique or just old tools and farm implements.

Now, leave the oven alone, letting it bake for thirty minutes, or until the coals turn white and are no longer heating it. Then add more fresh coals from the fire, and, holding the entire Dutch oven by its handle, rotate it 180 degrees. This rotation prevents the food from becoming overcooked on the side facing the central fire. Turning the Dutch oven may be an optional step, depending on the proximity of the fire to the implement. In a large fireplace, the heat of the central cooking fire may not affect the oven's temperature, especially if the oven is "baking" on the far edge of the hearth.

When indicated in your recipe, test the food for doneness in the standard way, such as with a cake tester or by tapping the tops of the bread loaves. When removing or replacing the lid of the Dutch oven, be very careful not to drop ashes or coals on your food.

After your baking is completed, "turn off" the oven by removing its lid. This is a very important step. It not only helps to stop the baking action, but prevents moisture from accumulating on the underside of the lid and dripping onto your food, giving it a peculiar flavor. Next, move the bottom of the oven (food inside) away from the coals and fire. When the food is cool, lift out your Dutch-oven-baked treat and enjoy your creation!

After you have mastered the basic routine just outlined for baking in your Dutch oven, you may want to try some of the following interesting variations on its use.

If you own two Dutch ovens, one preferably smaller than the other, you can bake in both of them simultaneously by stacking the smaller one on top of the larger. Baking in this double oven not only requires fewer coals (the coals on the lower lid serve to heat the bottom of the upper oven) and uses less hearth space, but allows you to bake desserts and bread at the same time. For ease in checking the progress of the baking, be sure to place the food with the longest cooking time in the bottom oven.

One can also bake successfully in a Dutch oven without using a cake pan or rack. The corn bread recipe included in the recipe section of this book turns out well prepared this way. Without a pan, the finished product has a rather free-form shape, but this doesn't diminish its flavor, quality, or ease in baking.

To bake directly on the bottom of your Dutch oven, you'll need to line it first either with leaves or heavy paper. For lack of paper, the early American housewife lined her oven with fresh maple leaves, when they were available. They left a pretty star-shaped pattern on the bottom of her baked goods, and the stems were natural handles for removing the lining when the baking was completed. In the dead of winter when the maple trees were bare, the more flexible leaves of a head of cabbage would do. In the fall, the housewife often sent her children a-leafing to collect maple leaves for use over the winter months. These were threaded on long strings and hung from the kitchen rafters to preserve them until they were needed.

Baking

Approximate Oven Temperatures and Distribution of Coals for Dutch Oven Baking

Biscuits. High heat. Evenly distribute an equal amount of coals on lid of oven and underneath it throughout baking.

Breads. Moderate to high heat. For first half of baking, evenly distribute an equal amount of coals on lid of oven and underneath it. For second half of baking, place slightly more coals on lid of oven to brown top crust.

Cakes. Moderate heat. Evenly distribute an equal amount of coals on lid of oven and underneath it throughout baking.

Cookies. High heat. Evenly distribute an equal amount of coals on lid of oven and underneath it throughout baking.

Custards. Moderate heat. Place slightly more coals on lid of oven than underneath it throughout baking.

Fruits. Moderate heat. Evenly distribute an equal amount of coals on lid of oven and underneath it throughout baking.

Muffins. Moderate heat. Evenly distribute an equal amount of coals on lid of oven and underneath it throughout baking.

Pies. Moderate to high heat. For first half of baking, place slightly more coals underneath oven than on top to set bottom crust. For second half of baking, reverse this, placing slightly more coals on lid of oven to brown top crust.

The modern housewife may want to stash some maple leaves in her freezer instead of hanging them from her ceiling, as we find this preserves them better. Although not as charming as maple leaves, several layers of brown paper cut from grocery bags to fit the oven's bottom and greased will also serve to line the Dutch oven effectively.

After lining the oven, pour or place your bread or cake mixture directly into it and proceed with the baking as described earlier. After the baking is completed, and the oven cool enough to handle, invert its bottom over a cutting board, allowing the baked foods to gently fall out. Carefully peel off the liner and you're ready to eat.

The Reflector Oven

The reflector bake oven, or tin kitchen, was another baking device American women used in their fireplaces. Introduced to the cooking hearth after the Dutch oven, it was supposedly an improvement over its predecessor. But it never gained the same degree of popularity for baking. This was probably

41

because these new ovens were considered an "extra" by the generally frugal housewives who already owned a very adequate and indestructible iron Dutch oven. And, in practice, not only did the reflector oven not bake quite as evenly as the Dutch oven, but it was not as versatile a cooking device. A cook could stew, fry, boil, bake, and perform most every cooking technique, except roasting, in her Dutch oven, while with a reflector bake oven she was limited to baking.

Tin kitchens or reflector ovens modified for roasting, on the other hand, were quickly accepted in the open-hearth kitchen, and were hailed by food authorities as the ultimate roasting device for fireplace cooking. The only difference between reflector ovens for roasting and those for baking was that the former were fitted with spits for suspending meat rather than with a shelf for holding breads, pies, cakes and other baked goods.

Unlike the Dutch oven, which is still being produced for campers and is available from many outlets including the Boy Scouts of America, the reflector bake oven is a scarce commodity. Antique versions are rare and expensive, and, while reproductions for camping use are reasonably priced, antique copies are dear.

But, if you are at all handy, it is not too difficult to build a reflector oven. Plans for constructing one have appeared in the magazine, *Early American Life*. To obtain these instructions, see Chapter 10. For a description of how to improvise a reflector bake oven from aluminum foil and other common household materials see *Backcountry Cooking*, by J. Wayne Fears, published by the East Woods Press.

Reflector oven baking.

Baking

The reflector bake oven, difficult as it may be to obtain, does offer some special advantages over the Dutch oven for the modern fireplace cook. For these reasons we have included a discussion of its use in this section. The reflector oven's plusses are: It does not need to be preheated before baking can begin, and it does not rely on coals to supply the baking heat. These factors speed the time when cooking can begin. The reflector oven takes up less hearth space than the Dutch oven, an important consideration with today's generally smaller fireplaces. It is lighter in weight than the Dutch oven, hence easier to handle. And it is cleaner to use, since its use involves no shoveling of ashes or coals before or after baking, a decisive factor if your fireplace happens to be in an elegant setting.

The modern-day reflector oven and its nineteenth-century antecedent work on the same principle. They rely on the reflected and direct heat of the fire to bake their foods. Both models are constructed of shiny metal (tin) to promote the greatest reflection of the fire's heat from their walls onto the food. The modern, although not widely available, camping version of the reflector bake oven resembles a large V resting on its side. It has small feet and an interior central shelf for holding the food. The original fireplace reflector ovens were shaped like cylinders sliced in half lengthwise, but they too had small feet and a shelf spanning their midsections.

To bake in these ovens, just put your dough or batter into a pan and place it on the oven's shelf; if you are baking cookies or biscuits, they may be set directly on the shelf; and the shelf may be greased or not as your recipes direct for the preparation of the cookie sheet or baking pan. Then place the oven, open end facing the fire, on the hearth floor about eight to ten inches from the heat to bake. This distance varies depending on the intensity of the fire and the reflecting ability of the oven's walls. A dirty oven, or an old one that has lost its shine, will not bake as efficiently as a bright, new one.

To judge the temperature, or readiness of the fire for reflector oven baking, here is a variation on the bare arm method used by the beehive oven bakers, from the Boy Scout handbook.

> Place your hand over the fire, and count in the following fashion: "one and one, two and two, etc." When you can no longer hold your hand over the heat, gauge the fire's temperature according to the following chart:
>
> Hand removed at a count of:
>
> | | |
> |---|---|
> | 6 – 8 | low (250 degrees) |
> | 4 – 5 | medium (350 – 400 degrees) |
> | 2 – 3 | hot (400-450 degrees) |
> | 1 or less | very hot (450 – 500 degrees) |

It is very important when using a reflector oven to check the progress of the baking food frequently. This is most easily and safely accomplished by very gently pulling the oven away from the fire, with pot-holder-protected hands, for a quick look at the food. To raise or lower the baking temperature, one has only to move the oven closer to or further away from the heat.

Test your baking food for doneness in the conventional way at the time indicated in your recipe. When your cooking is completed, move the oven a comfortable distance away from the fire and remove the bread, cookies, etc., to a rack to cool.

If you really like this baking technique, and if your fireplace is large enough, next try baking in two reflector ovens at one time. Place the ovens on the hearth so that they face one another with the cooking fire built between them. Lay the fire sideways so that the oven openings are in front of the tunnel opening formed by stacked logs. Place uncooked food on shelves of both ovens and allow to bake. Follow tips outlined above for baking in a single reflector oven.

Two ovens, used as described, are supposed to be super-efficient, multiplying the potential surfaces for the fire's heat to reflect and deflect from, and thereby increasing their baking actions.

The Hanging Griddle

If you are lucky enough to already have a crane or an adjustable trammel in your fireplace, or are thinking about installing either of them, then you can also try baking on a griddle. Early American bake griddles were round, flat iron plates with large curved handles and swivel hooks by which the cook suspended them over the fire to bake her food. The swivel hook allowed the cook to turn the griddle baking surface in order to even out its heat and to easily bring all of the baking food within her reach. Some versions of the bake griddle had short feet so that it would also rest firmly on the fireplace floor. And still other models were constructed so that they were collapsible. The baking surface in these was hinged so that it folded into the same plane as the handle when not in use.

Griddle baking was an interesting baking method and one that has fallen into disuse in our modern kitchens. One of the few remnants of this technique which still remains today is the practice of baking pancakes in our frying pans. But griddle baking had obvious limitations, even in early American homes. It would, for example be hard to imagine baking a layer cake or a hearty loaf of bread on a griddle. Its areas of best use were in the preparation of small baked goods: cookies, biscuits, muffins, and cupcakes.

Antique bake griddles were widely used on cooking hearths, and are still plentiful in antique shops today. Reproductions of this implement though, are

"Baking" pancakes on the hanging griddle. French toast, bannocks, and English muffins can be baked this way at your hearth.

not being mass produced, to our knowledge, so one would have to commission a blacksmith to make a copy for you, if in your travels you did not uncover an authentic one.

Here's how to bake on the griddle. Hang it from the crane or trammel so that its baking plate sits about 1½ to 2 feet above the logs of a well-established cooking fire. The griddle should not hang in the fire's flames. Preheat the griddle in this position for about ten minutes. When it's hot, place your biscuit dough or other unbaked food on it. Let the food bake undisturbed for the length of time indicated in the recipe, turn, if necessary, and then remove a sample with a metal spatula or tongs to test for doneness. Be careful not to tip the griddle when you are performing this last step or you will have made ash cakes. During baking you may need to adjust the height of the griddle in order to increase or decrease the baking temperature. Different lengths of pothooks or an adjustment in the trammel will accomplish this. The cook may also have to turn the griddle if one area of the baking surface is hotter than another.

Baking "rings" were a common accessory used on baking griddles during the fireplace cooking period. Small rings about 1½ inches in diameter and 1 inch high, they were forms for containing the more liquid batters baked on the griddle. These rings can easily be improvised in a few moments from several thicknesses of heavy aluminum foil folded into one-inch strips with their ends pinched, clipped, or stapled together to form a circle. Empty seven-ounce tuna or salmon cans with their bottoms as well as their tops removed can also serve as baking rings.

The Waffle and Wafer Iron

Waffle and wafer irons were common accessories in early American fireplaces. They produced delicious baked desserts that were consumed with great relish at the hearth (often as fast as the cook could make them), and were served topped or filled with sweetened fruit or jam and whipped cream, or dipped in honey. Both the waffle and wafer iron cooked batter or dough by pressing it between two preheated, patterned iron plates that were hinged together. These plates were attached to long handles, which enabled the cook to heat the irons at a comfortable distance from the fire and allowed her to extract them safely and easily when they reached the appropriate temperature for baking.

Waffle irons were designed to hold a looser batter then wafer irons. They were usually rectangular or round, although some were heart-shaped, and their baking surfaces were cast in a deep grid design, the traditional waffle pattern. The light, crispy, cake-like waffles baked in them were comparable to those we eat today.

By comparison, wafer iron baking plates were usually round or rectangular and their baking surfaces were decorated with a variety of delicate designs. Commonly pictured were birds, flowers, hearts, a bride's initials, or even religious motifs, since theses irons were also used to make wafers for sacramental purposes. Unlike waffle irons, the baking surfaces of the wafer iron were essentially flat, as these patterns were only shallowly incised. A small, stiff ball of sweetened dough (or a finger of dough, depending on the iron's shape) was pressed between its two plates, as a more liquid batter would have run off its shallow surfaces. The resulting wafers resembled thin, crispy, and very pretty cookies.

Preheating waffle iron in coals.

Waffle iron with cooked waffle. Gridiron or green log is good to rest waffle or wafer iron on to remove baked product.

Like most antiques, authentic waffle and wafer irons are scarce. Especially coveted by collectors are the more ornately decorated ones. So your chances of finding one of theses irons at a reasonable price are rather remote. But similar baking irons are still being used and produced by other cultures around the world, and these can be used in your fireplace, although their manufacturers generally include directions for their use only on modern cooktops. A Belgian waffle iron with non-stick coating on its baking surface and a temperature gauge, and an Italian pizzelle iron for making fluted wafers, were both offered in recent Williams-Sonoma catalogues, an excellent mail-order source for unusual cooking equipment. Similar irons can also probably be found in a well-stocked gourmet or kitchen supplies shop or in the housewares section of larger department stores such as Bloomingdale's.

Using a waffle or wafer iron is surprisingly simple. First you must season its cooking surfaces by rubbing them with a coating of vegetable oil or shortening. Next, the iron is preheated by resting it for a few minutes over a healthy bed of glowing coals or on the top log of the cooking fire. It should take about three to five minutes to preheat the iron, and it should be turned over midway during the heating process so both sides of the iron are equally heated. (A drop of water will sizzle on the cooking surface of the iron when it is ready for baking.) Next, remove the iron from the fire, and rest it on a trivet or log near the edge of the hearth. Open it, and add your batter (for a waffle) or ball of dough (for a wafer). Close the iron and let it "cook" undisturbed until steam stops coming out its sides, another two to three minutes. This time will vary depending on the size of the iron and the temperature of its baking surface.

Then open the iron, being careful not to burn your fingers, and gently pry the wafer or waffle away from the sides of the iron with the tines of a fork or the tip of a sharp knife, and serve. For wafers, many early American recipes suggest rolling the cookie while it is still warm and pliable, and then filling it when cool, with whipped cream, and adding a bit of jam or a fresh strawberry at either end to serve as a decorative and tasty stopper. Repeat for each waffle and wafer desired, until your mixture is used up.

The amount of dough or batter to use for each waffle and wafer will be determined largely by the size of your iron. You will have to experiment a little to come up with an exact measurement. Usually for a standard-sized and –shaped wafer iron, a ball of dough the size of a walnut is adequate, and for a waffle iron about ⅛-cup of batter will suffice. It is better to estimate slightly less for your first trials, as overflowing batter will make quite a mess on your hearth. Reseason the iron as needed—usually after every three or four waffles or wafers is often enough.

Indian-Style Baking

Last but not least, we feel we can't omit a short mention of the simplest of all baking techniques, baking food right in the fire's hot coals, Indian-style.

As we observed earlier, Indian-style is not a satisfactory technique for baking cakes, pies, breads, or baked goods in general. Almost any other basic food, however, can be easily and tastily prepared in this way. The possibilities are really endless, from baked apples to baked chicken. Indian-style baking is also a technique that children can participate in and will enjoy. And it can provide the inspiration for an Indian birthday party lunch, an imaginative and delicious alternative to fast food.

To prepare foods for baking in the coals, replace the green corn husks, cabbage leaves, and parchment, which the Indians and our first settlers used for wrapping their foods, with aluminum foil.

Select basic foods to cook in this manner. Acorn squash, ears of corn, yams, or chicken legs would be good choices. Add butter and seasonings as your tastes dictate. Then wrap small amounts or individual portions of the food carefully in several layers of foil, sealing the edges well. Next, sit the packages on a layer of hot coals to cook, placing a few more coals on the tops of these packages, as well, so that tops and bottoms bake evenly.

When the food is finished cooking, or when you are checking its progress by slitting the top of the package or carefully unwrapping it, take care not to pierce the bottom layer of foil as you will lose all the delicious juices inside. A spatula or wooden tongs are good tools for this last step.

Now sit cross-legged, Indian-style, around the fire and feast!

4

Roasting, Toasting, Broiling, and Browning Off

To most modern Americans nurtured on food cooked with gas, electricity, and microwaves, one of the unexpected and unparalleled delights of fireplace cooking is that food broiled, toasted, but most especially roasted before a wood fire develops a pleasing and unique flavor. It's a flavor that has never been equaled by any other more advanced cooking method, fuel, or device—the charcoal barbecue included.

Early American housewives took this benefit rather lightly, or perhaps they were just exhausted from the backbreaking labor required of their ground-level hearths—the standard design of most cooking fireplaces that were built in this country. Whatever the most compelling reason, American women (the ones who could afford to) readily abandoned their kitchen fireplaces for the revolutionary wood-burning cookstoves introduced in the early 1800s. It is amusing to interject here that a few staunch supporters of the flavor of fireplace-cooked food were convinced that these new-fangled devices would never gain broad acceptance. Food prepared on them simply didn't taste as good as when it was prepared in the old-fashioned manner, at the hearth.

Although there was a lot of truth to such claims, these voices were very much in the minority, and were most likely not those of the household cooks. As history has recorded, progress prevailed, and the American fascination for kitchen gadgetry produced dramatically new methods of mechanized meal preparation. An overwhelming array of devices, designed to improve and simplify our lives, have all but engulfed our kitchens, and have pressed wood as a cooking fuel into virtual extinction. While we are not suggesting that you toss your modern conveniences into the garbage and resurrect a fireplace for everyday cooking, we do feel there is something to be enjoyed and gained by following some of the cooking techniques of the past that we have been too quick to discard as outmoded. This is especially true for roasting.

In many European countries, by comparison, and in more exotic parts of the world as well, roasting with a wood fire has remained through the years a highly regarded cooking technique and one which is still practiced in many private homes and in some of the finest restaurants. And, only lately, a growing interest and sophistication about food among Americans has prompted in our more cosmopolitan cities the appearance of restaurants where true roasting has been revived, and where one can experience the delectable flavor of food cooked before a wood fire.

Roasting In Early America

Historically, fireplace cooks defined roasting quite differently from the way we define it today. In fact, early cooking authorities would have considered our modern method of roasting more like baking. Today, the meat is placed in the oven, resting on a rack in a shallow pan, with a small amount of water covering the bottom. This is described as a procedure for preparing a plain baked dish, one which is suitable for the family table.

Fireplace era roasting was described in 1770 by Martha Bradley, author of *The British Housewife*, a book known to have been circulated in the Colonies, as "dressing food before a naked fire." Positioning food directly over flames or coals to be roasted was not desirable, as it allowed dripping fat and juices from the meat to fall on the fire or coals. This produced billowing smoke and spitting flames that engulfed the food, affected its flavor, and irritated the cook's eyes.

Early food writers were also quite specific in their directions regarding the quality and preparations necessary for good roasting fire. To quote Eliza Leslie: "A roasting fire should be prepared at least one half hour before the roast is put down." (From our own experience, more like forty-five minutes is needed to allow for the less proficient fire-building skills of the modern cook.) "It (the fire)," she continued, "should be large, steady, clear, and bright with plenty of fine hot coals at the bottom." "Your (roasting) fire must also be made in proportion to the piece you are to dress...," wrote Susannah Carter. And fireplace cooks generally agreed that a large blaze filling the entire hearth accomplished nothing except to overheat the cook and the room. The location of the fire on the hearth was also commented upon. The best spot for roasting (remember, these references are to the oversized, often cavernous cooking fireplaces of yesterday) was near the front of the fireplace and off to one side of it. Here, the roast could be easily reached for turning and basting without its presence interfering with the housewife's other cooking activities.

Fireplace era cookbooks also offered early cooks a number of guidelines to follow when preparing their meat for roasting. These directions are summarized below. They apply to roasting beef in particular, but they were also applicable to a leg of lamb, whole turkey, and even a haunch of venison. A few of these suggestions may seem curious and puzzling to the modern reader, but many of the others are still very relevant for fireplace roasting today. Still, they are included here more for their historical interest than for their practical importance.

Washing meat in cold water, wiping it dry, and rubbing it with salt were Eliza Leslie's method of preparing a roast for the spit. Even then, however, the application of salt before cooking commenced was controversial. Other early food writers warned that salting meat too soon in the cooking process drew out its juices and ruined the roast, an opinion held by many cooks today.

Another roasting practice of early cooks was to tie blank paper over the fat of the roast. The purpose of the paper covering was to prevent that fat from melting away, or "wasting too fast," the old cooks said.

Care was also taken to position the roast at the proper distance from the fire. The outside of the meat could become burned before the inside was cooked if it was placed too close to the heat (good, practical advice that holds true today, as well).

Twenty minutes per pound was used by chefs of the later fireplace cooking era to estimate the length of time to roast their meat. Cooking time, naturally, varied with the size of the roast, with the tastes (for rare or well-done meat) of the diners, and curiously enough, with the season of the year. In summer, it was observed, a roast cooked faster than in the winter months. This is a point the authors will accept at face value, as we don't intend to verify this information by preparing a fireplace meal on a typical, eighty-five degree, humid, New Jersey August day.

Another interesting observation of early cooks was that steam from the roast "drew" towards the fire when the roast was done. Such information was probably more useful for the homemaker before cooking timers, scales, and oven thermometers were at her disposal.

And finally, another widespread practice that has fallen out of use today was for cooks to dredge a roast lightly with flour and a little melted butter when its cooking neared completion. This produced a delicate froth on the surface of the meat which supposedly enhanced its appearance.

To suspend, support, and rotate the haunches of venison, hindquarters of bear, whole 'coons, woodchucks, wild turkeys, and the meat of the other wild and domesticated animals that were roasted in American fireplaces, many ingenious and elaborate devices were invented and used by early cooks. Some of these roasting aides even incorporated their own dripping pans, reflecting panels, and turning mechanisms.

The simplest of these roasting implements, and one which can be easily duplicated and used today, was improvised from only a long length of stout cord or a thin strip of rawhide. Using one end of the cord, the cook trussed her fowl or tied her piece of meat into a neat and secure package. She then tied the other end of this cord to a nail or hook in the fireplace mantel or chimney throat so that the food hung directly in front of a hot fire. An occasional prod with her large meat fork caused the cord to wind and then unwind on itself. The motion exposed all sides of the food to the fire, browning and cooking it evenly with very little attention from the chef.

The cord method, as well as all the other devises used to roast food in the fireplace, with the exception of the tin kitchen, required that a pan be placed under the cooking meat to catch its dripping fat and juices. These pans, called dripping pans, served a dual purpose. They not only prevented fat from accumulating on the hearth and perhaps causing a serious fire, but they also collected the drippings, which the cook used to baste her roasting food, and the grease, which was saved to make rush lights and candles.

While roasting with a hanging cord was simple and effective, its major drawback was that one could not cook on a string the abundant and delicate-fleshed fish that this country's settlers enjoyed and often relied upon for survival. To roast fish, the earliest fireplace cooks resorted instead to a technique known as "planking." Copied from the American Indians cooking, planking involved tying the whole fish or its fillets to a slab of hard, preferably fruit or nut wood. This improvised cooking sheet was then propped at an angle before the fire to roast the food. A heavy object such as log, stone, or iron pot was used to support the plank in the desired position.

This procedure works as well today as it did yesterday for all kinds of fish, a food which, in general, cooks rather quickly. But it was inadequate then, as now, for roasting the denser, slower-cooking flesh of domestic livestock and wild game, since after a prolonged period before the fire, the plank began to roast along with the food.

An improvement over these two primitive methods–the cord and the plank–was the spit. A fireplace utensil versatile enough for roasting both meat and fish, it became the standard roasting implement for the fireplace cook.

The first spits, used in the poorest homes and in the most primitive settings, were probably just sturdy green branches with one end sharpened to a point to spear the roasting food. The cook either held this spit in her hand while cooking dinner or anchored it at an angle before the fire with rocks. Roasting in this manner is familiar to scouts and campers, who still use this method of

cooking at campsites. But for daily fireplace cooking, it was at best a makeshift arrangement. The branch could support only small pieces of food, and the cook ran the risk of her spit burning and breaking before her cooking was completed.

As blacksmiths became more common, branch spits were replaced with iron ones, the simplest of which closely resembled the sharpened branch just described. These spits were forged, spear-like pieces of iron two to three feet in length, with two short feet that supported the spit in an unbalanced seesaw position before the fire. The food was impaled on the raised end of the spit. Although generally very crudely formed, sometimes the handle ends of these spits were embellished by a creative blacksmith with fanciful designs or formed into a heart or other decorative shape. But while the iron version of the branch spit had the advantage of not catching fire as did its antecedent, it still could hold only smaller pieces of food before the fire, and it sometimes became extremely hot and hard to handle.

A major improvement on the iron spear spit was the horizontal iron spit. The horizontal iron spit could support large cuts of meat, as well as fish, and also permitted the cook to turn them with ease before the fire. The horizontal iron spit was supported before the fire on hooks which protruded from vertical sections of special cooking andirons. A series of hook-rests were attached at different levels on the verticals of the andirons to allow the cook to raise or lower the spit, adjusting its distance from the fire and the cooking temperature of the food. Most fireplace kitchens were equipped with several iron spits in varying lengths and thicknesses from which the cook selected one appropriate for the size of her roast.

Another, more unusual, way of suspending the horizontal roasting spit in the fireplace can be observed at Hopewell Village in Elverson, Pennsylvania. Hopewell Village was a major iron-forging community in the 1700s, and has been restored to its former appearance and designated as a National Historic Site. In this recreated eighteenth-century setting, food is roasted over glowing coals by resting either end of an iron spit in two very long (about sixteen-inch) pot or S hooks hung from the crane. This is a practice that fits in with the custom of building a cooking fire without andirons that was common to the settlers of certain sections of Pennsylvania, as mentioned in Chapter 2, The Cooking Fire.

A large fish was splinted with sticks and tied to these horizontal spits. A cut of meat or whole fowl was pierced through its cavity, or thickest part, and then skewered and tied to the spit to hold it in place while it roasted. One end of these spits was usually bent by the blacksmith to serve as a handle for turning the roasting food more easily.

A refinement of the standard spit design was the basket or cradle spit.

Basket spits were simply modified, standard spits in which the spit's center was intersected by a large ovoid metal basket, or cage-like compartment. In this basket, the cook placed fragile-fleshed foods, such as fish, before the fire to roast. The basket simplified the process of attaching these foods to the spit by eliminating splinting and trying. They also helped to preserve the food's shape and appearance for serving, and prevented juices from escaping, since a basket spit did not pierce the skin or flesh of the roasting food.

While these simple, yet satisfactory methods (cord, plank and spit) enabled the fireplace cook to roast her foods to perfection, and to ensure even cooking, they did require that she or someone else be in constant attendance to baste and turn the roasting food. Whenever possible the cook assigned her children to the task of sitting by the fire and patiently turning the roast, not an unpleasant job in the freezing winter months. In England, often poor children were paid a small sum to perform this job. They were called turnspits. When manpower was unavailable, sometimes even dogs were recruited to turn the spit. Specially trained for the task, these animals walked in a cage on a treadmill which activated a system of gears causing the spitted meat to rotate before the fire. Canine spits were first used in Tudor England and later brought to the Colonies.

But the best solution to this problem was the invention of mechanisms called jacks to turn the roasting food automatically. These jacks included the commonly used clock jack, the less frequently seen smoke jack, and the even rarer steam jack.

A smoke jack, interestingly enough, was designed by Leonardo da Vinci in the fifteenth century, but not introduced to the American hearth until the eighteenth century. Also called a chimney wheel because of its appearance and location, the smoke jack was installed in the chimney throat, where it utilized the updraft of hot air from the fire to turn its fan-shaped blades. The resultant windmill effect caused a series of connecting gears and chains to turn the spitted food, roasting it evenly without so much as a glance or prod from the cook.

In the late 1700s a steam jack was patented by John Bailey of New York City. In this unusual device, steam generated by the heat of the fire was harnessed to turn the roasting spit. But steam jacks were either impractical or didn't work very well, and few were manufactured.

The most commonly used jacks in the American fireplace were the clock jacks. These did not rely for their energy on the unpredictable pressure of the chimney's updraft or on the varying heat of the fire to produce a steady supply of steam. Developed during Charles II's reign as King of England, clock jacks, like the rarer jacks described above, appeared on the American hearth in the eighteenth century. In its simplest version, the clock jack utilized a tightly coiled clock spring mechanism to turn the roasting food. This jack resembled an ordinary wooden potato masher or bottle, and is sometimes referred to as a bottle jack. It was usually made of brass, and a long chain and hook hung from it to which the cook attached her roast. The masher or bottle-shaped case held the clock spring mechanism, which the cook wound with a key. As the spring mechanism unwound it caused the chain and the meat to revolve before the fire.

Another more complicated and perhaps earlier version of the clock jack was often called a gravity jack, since it translated the energy created by dropping a weight or weights to turn the roasting spit. It worked on a principle similar to that of tall case clocks. The cook wound the weights of the gravity clock jack with a crank attached to a flywheel. As the weights slowly dropped, the energy released turned a series of gears, connected to a rope, a pulley, and finally to the spit.

By far the best all-around device developed for roasting during the fireplace cooking period was not the manual or automatic spit, but the reflector oven. These were similar to the reflector baking ovens described in the preceding chapter. The reflector roasting oven was a cylindrical shiny box on legs, with a large opening on one side to expose the roasting food to the fire. Not only was it lightweight, but it combined in a single unit all the best features of the other roasting implements. Incorporated in this ingenious device were an adjustable spit with skewer, dripping pan with spout, reflecting panels, a hinged door for checking the roast's progress and for basting it, handles for moving the oven, and in its most refined models, small hooks on the underside of its top edge from which the cook hung pieces of food to roast too small to be threaded on the central spit.

Unquestionably the *pièce de résistance* of fireplace roasting apparatus, the tin kitchen remains as impressive a device today as it was yesterday. It is still useful even in our generally smaller modern fireplaces that are often surrounded by carpeting and finished floors, where neatness and compactness are especially important. And while antique examples of this implement are rare and extremely expensive, reproductions can be ordered from many private tinsmiths and through the catalogs and museum shops of the larger restorations. Chapter 10, Sources for Hearth Cookware and Accessories, lists a number of outlets for reflector roasting ovens.

In addition to the tin kitchen and the basic horizontal spit, many other specialty roasting devices were developed for fireplace cooking. One of these was the bird-roaster or oven. Essentially, this device was only a smaller, simpler tin kitchen. A small, free-standing, L-shaped piece of tin, the bird roaster was equipped with sharp hooks that protruded from the vertical, reflecting panel. From these hooks the cook hung songbirds—a commonly consumed delicacy on the early American table–or other small pieces of meat that she wished to roast. The bottom, or horizontal, half of the oven served as a support and as a pan to catch the drippings from the roasting morsels. Some bird ovens had drip pan inserts with spouts.

Another roasting device, seen less frequently on the American hearth, was the English roasting frame. It resembled an instrument of torture more than a cooking tool. From a tall, vertical shaft of iron which stood on three legs protruded a series of sharp, dangerous looking spikes. On these spikes, the cook impaled the food she desired to roast, placing the frame in front of the fire's heat. Below the meat spikes, a circular ring of metal held a removable basin which caught the drippings.

Coffee roasters were another interesting group of devices which were developed for the fireplace. These roasters were of two general designs. In the first group, a long iron rod with a pointed end had a cylindrical metal compartment with a sliding or hinged door attached near the pointed end for holding raw coffee beans. To roast the beans, the cook held the roaster and twirled it as one would an umbrella, its pointed end on the hearth floor, near enough to the fire to heat the beans. The other general type of coffee roaster was a self-supporting unit. The coffee bean compartment in this unit rested on a special rack under which coals were placed. The cook turned a crank or handle attached to the end of the coffee bean container to rotate it for even roasting of the beans inside.

Yet another group of roasting accessories for the fireplace were popcorn and chestnut roasters. They both worked on the same basic principle, and are made much the same in design today as they were in early America. In most of these roasters, basket-like compartments made of wire or pierced metal held the kernels of corn or nuts. These were attached to long wooden or metal handles so that the cook could hold the basket at a comfortable distance from the fire or over its coals while the corn popped or the nuts roasted. A common mistake, by the way, made today when popping corn or roasting nuts in the fireplace, is to place the basket in the fire's flame. This practice tends to char and burn the corn and nuts before they have had a chance to pop or roast properly.

Techniques For Today

There are four methods of roasting food that we have found particularly suitable to today's fireplaces. For meat, these techniques are: hanging the roast or fowl by a length of butcher's twine; skewering the meat on a new horizontal spit (either one made expressly for the fireplace use, or a barbecue spit modified for this purpose); roasting the meat in a reproduction tin kitchen; and planking, the best method for cooking fish. We have included planking in the roasting category since the cooking is performed before the fire.

The Hanging Cord

Roasting food by hanging it in front of the fire on a cord is an especially easy and inexpensive technique. It requires only a few yards of heavy cotton or butcher's twine from your butcher, or from a 5 & 10 or hardware store. Using about three yards of this material, truss or tie your meat or fowl in a secure package. Do not cut off the leftover piece of cord, but attach it to a nail in your fireplace mantel, to the damper handle, or even to the crane, adjusting the cord so that the roast hangs directly in front of the fire. Be sure to choose a tying place that allows the meat to fall fairly close to the fire (about five inches in front is desirable), and low enough so that it hangs directly in front of the tunnel formed by the log configuration of the cooking fire. This position will give the roast the full benefit of the fire's intensity. Next, place a dripping pan

Roasting a duck on a length of butcher's twine. Other foods, such as a chicken, goose, and leg of lamb can be roasted this way as well. Be sure to place a generous-sized pan under the cooking food to catch the drippings. (String is tied to nail in mantle.)

under the roast, and reflecting panels in front of it. Reflecting panels are optional, but are easily made in a few moments (see the illustration on page 60). Their use makes maximum use of the energy of the fire by reflecting its heat onto the side of the roast opposite the fire, and will cook your food rapidly and evenly.

As the meat roasts, occasionally prod it with a large meat fork. This will cause the cord to wind up, and, as it unwinds, to turn the roast, exposing all sides of it to the fire. (If you don't use reflecting panels, keeping the roast turning is especially important.) Also baste the meat with pan drippings whenever you think of it.

To ensure even cooking, and after the roast is about half done, turn it so that the uppermost part, which is generally somewhat cooler, now points down toward the hearth, where it is exposed to the fire's fullest intensity. The easiest way to accomplish this switch is to have a friend support the roasting food on a plate to relieve the considerable tension on the cord. Next, cut the slack cord at the point where it is joined to the roast and retie it to the trussing string on the other end of the roast. Then remove the plate and continue roasting until the food is done.

We usually determine doneness by inserting an instant meat thermometer when we anticipate that the meat is nearly cooked based on weight of the roast. But a conventional meat thermometer could be used as well, by inserting it before the roasting process commences. For smaller fowl—chicken, ducks, Cornish hens—we don't bother with a meat thermometer at all, since doneness can accurately be judged by cutting into a joint, twisting a leg, or any of the other regular methods of checking a fowl to detect whether or not it is cooked adequately. For turkeys, which are usually considerably larger than other roasting fowls, we make an exception to this rule, and recommend that you use a meat thermometer or purchase prepared roasting turkeys with the button that pops up when they are cooked. Some of the larger roasting chickens are now packaged with these handy indicators, as well.

The Roasting Spit

One of the most practical ways of roasting meat in your fireplace is on a horizontal spit. In the interest of economy a spit is most cheaply devised by having a blacksmith make a new one for you out of a length of square bar stock, and a pair of brackets or tripods to support it out of angle iron. The brackets should be designed so that the spit can be supported at different levels before the fire for temperature control. The spit's thickness should be selected to permit the modern "U" shaped rotisserie or barbecue skewers, with wing nuts for tightening them to the spit, readily found in hardware stores, to slide along its length. These skewers are the best gadgets we have found for holding meat on a spit. Any competent and fairly imaginative blacksmith could fabricate such a combination for you.

If you want to add an authentic period look and feel to your roasting activities, nothing is more impressive than good reproductions of old cooking andirons, spits and skewer. Most blacksmiths and other craftsmen will make handsome reproductions of these implements for you, although the expense will be considerably greater than that of the simpler spit and bracket arrangement just described. Also keep in mind that when using cooking andirons, you will have to lay your cooking firewood directly on them, rather than on the fireplace floor.

To roast your meat on a spit, season it as your recipe directs, and if it is a fowl, truss it with cotton string or butcher's twine, as well. Then thread the spit through the thickest part of the meat, or poke it through the cavity of the fowl, and skewer it very securely in place so that when the spit is rotated, the meat turns along with it. Next, rest the spit on the brackets or cooking andirons so that the roast sits directly in front of the tunnel of the cooking fire. Here it receives the full benefit of the fire's heat. Place a dripping pan under the food and reflecting panels in front of it. Let the roast cook, occasionally basting and turning it, so that it browns nicely on all sides. Test for doneness with a meat thermometer, or by any of the other methods mentioned above in the discussion on roasting with a hanging cord.

To adjust the roasting temperature when cooking food on the improvised bracket supports, the cook has the options of either raising or lowering the spit in front of the fire, or of moving the brackets holding the spit closer to or further away from the fire.

The Tin Kitchen

The tin kitchen is in reality nothing more than an embellished spit with all of its accessories attached, and the procedure for roasting in it is exactly the same as the procedure for using an ordinary spit. With the tin kitchen, unlike the spit, temperature control can be achieved only by moving the entire oven closer to, or further away from, the fire. To maximize the oven's roasting potential, be sure to keep the interior reflecting surfaces bright and shiny. If you are using an old oven that has lost its shine, lining it with aluminum foil will recreate the effect of the tin-coated surfaces.

The main advantage to using a tin kitchen over the simple spit is that this device is essentially spatterproof, since the cooking meat is shielded on three

Suckling pig roasting on a spit before the fire. Oven liners make good reflecting panels when fastened together with screws. When used as shown they greatly improve the cooking efficiency of the fire.

Cornish hens roasting in a nineteenth-century tin kitchen. Aluminum foil is used to line the oven to improve the reflecting ability of the worn metal.

sides by the reflecting panels of the oven. This is an important consideration if your fireplace is located in a setting where spattered grease would be difficult or impossible to remove.

There are several drawbacks to using a tin kitchen, however. One is that its normal size limits the number of chickens, ducks, etc., that you can cook at once. Also antique tin kitchens are exceedingly rare, and among the most expensive of the period roasting devices, and they are frequently found with some essential part missing or broken. Reproductions are available from a number of restorations and independent tinsmiths, but these copies are expensive, as well.

Planking a Fish

Planking is a simple and inexpensive way of roasting a fish in your fireplace. The procedure requires little more than a flat, clean board of hardwood large enough to hold the fish you want to cook. If you don't have a piece of hardwood handy, a board of softwood covered with aluminum foil, shiny side up, will do. The foil keeps the softer wood from catching fire, which it will do more readily than the hardwoods, and prevents the food from picking up an unpleasant flavor caused by direct contact with the resins of many softwoods, especially pine.

To plank a whole fish, prepare it as your recipe directs, seasoning and/or stuffing it. Then place it on the wood roasting sheet and place fat rolls of alu-

A whole fish can be planked, too. Instead of nailing it to the plank, tie it securely with sturdy string or butcher's twine. A stuffed fish is placed belly side up before the fire first to set the filling. It is also helpful to put a roll of foil or a dowel of wood (2 wooden spoons will do) next to each side of the fish to relieve the pressure from the string and prevent it from cutting into the soft flesh of the fish.

Fish fillet nailed to plank roasting before the fire.

minum foil, slightly thicker than the fish, along either side of it. (The purpose of the foil is to relieve the stress of the cord binding the fish to the board, and prevents it from cutting into the skin and flesh of the fish as it cooks.) Next, tie the fish to the plank by winding butcher's twine around it and the board, a number of times. Prop the fish up horizontally with a brick, log, or pot before the fire to roast. If it is stuffed, place the cavity opening up, an extra precaution against the fillings dripping out. When the fish is done on the side exposed to the fire, it should be flopped, or turned over, on the plank, so that both sides can cook evenly. To accomplish this, simply untie the string, turn the fish with spatulas, and replace the foil rolls and string. Continue to roast until the other side is cooked.

To test the fish for doneness, pierce its flesh with the tip of a sharp knife or the tines of a fork. The flesh should flake easily when it is cooked. To serve: remove the string and rolls of foil, and garnish the fish right on the plank with lemon wedges, sprigs of fresh parsley, and, if your board is large enough, any accompanying vegetables. Present the garnished fish to your guests and serve it right from this innovative platter.

To roast fish fillets on a plank, attach them to the board with nails instead of twine. Most any common nails will do. They should be clean, of medium thickness and at least 1 inch long. Place the fillets on the board, skin side down, and barely hammer the nails into the board through the edges of the fillets, so that they are easy to remove when the fish is cooked. Place nails all around the perimeter of the fish, spacing them about 1½ inches apart. Then, prop the planked fillets vertically in front of the fire to roast until done. There is no need to turn or "flop" fillets during cooking, as recommended for a whole fish, since they are so thin, but one may want to baste them to keep them from drying out. It may also be necessary to shift the position of the board so that the upper and lower parts of the fillets cook evenly. Test for doneness in the same way as for a whole fish. When cooking is completed, carefully remove nails with pliers, and serve the fillets garnished on the board as suggested above for a whole planked fish.

It is a good idea to save the planking board, so you don't have to scrounge around for another the next time you wish to plank a fish. Fruitwood boards additionally impart their fragrance to the fish.

Toasting, In Early America

As a cooking technique, toasting is much the same as roasting in that it uses the naked fire to cook food. The main differences between the two are the length of cooking time involved, and the foods generally cooked by this method. In general, toasting requires less cooking time than roasting, and it is a technique largely associated with bread or other baked goods, rather than with cuts of meat. Additionally, since toasting traditionally involves bread, drippings, which could cause the fire to smoke, are not produced during the cooking process. Hence, the cook is not limited when toasting to solely placing her food before the fire, as she is roasting. She can hold it over coals, or even over the burning fire, provided it's above the flames.

Toasting bread slices in an antique toaster. Slices must be turned to permit even browning.

63

To toast cheese and other thick foods that will not fit in your fireplace toaster, either toast them on a long-handled kitchen fork or rest them on a gridiron before the fire. Raclette is pictured here melting before the fire. The foil covering the gridiron catches cheese that melts before diners can catch it.

In early American fireplaces, food was either toasted by holding it in front of the fire or over its coals with a toasting fork, or by placing it in a fireplace toaster in front of the fire. Toasting forks were simply large two-pronged forks with long handles. Some of these oversized forks had short feet as well, so that they could sit on the hearth floor and toast food without the cook's help.

Regular fireplace toasters, also called down-hearth toasters, consisted of shallow wrought iron racks on short legs with a handle. They held one or two slices of bread before the fire. In the earliest fireplace toasters, the racks were stationary. To toast bread in these models, when one side of the bread was browned, the cook had to remove the slice and replace it, turning the untoasted side towards the fire. An improvement was for the toasting rack to revolve, so that with a nudge from her fork the cook could turn the uncooked side of the toast towards the fire. And in the later fireplace toasters, very long handles were hinged where they joined the racks, so that the cook did not even have to bend down to turn the roast—a twist of her wrist accomplished this maneuver instead.

Fireplace toasters were also among the most attractive of all the open-hearth cooking implements. The bars forming their wrought iron racks were often twisted and bent into ornate and delicate shapes, which left a brand or shadow on the toasted bread.

While toasting seems so simple and straightforward a process to us today, historically the rationale and procedure for toasting in America's cooking fireplaces was discussed at length, almost to the point of absurdity by some early cooks. Here is an example of these excesses from *The Boston Cook Book of 1883*:

> Bread is toasted...before the fire to extract the moisture and make it more palatable and digestible. If the slices be cut thick and carelessly exposed to a blazing fire, the outside is blackened and made into charcoal before the heat can reach the inside; the moisture is only heated, not evaporated, making the inside doughy...The correct way is to have the bread stale, and cut into thin uniform slices about one quarter of an inch thick.
>
> For toasting the bread...The fire should be clear, red (not blazing) coals. If you require only one or two slices, a toasting-fork will answer; but if a larger quantity be needed, there is nothing better than a double broiler.
>
> Bread properly dried and toasted is changed from the nature of dough, which always has a tendency to sour on the stomach, into pure wheat farina. It is not so scorched as to turn the butter into oil, but absorbs the butter; the butter and farina being easily separated, are quickly acted upon by the gastric fluid. Many persons prefer toast that is soft inside, but it should never be served to sick people in that manner.

Techniques for Today: The Toasting Fork, Fireplace Toaster, and Double Broiler

Toasting in one's fireplace is accomplished in much the same way today, as it was in the eighteenth century. In place of an antique toasting fork one can use a long barbecue fork with a wooden handle for toasting bread, muffins, and even marshmallows before the fire. Hold the fork so that the food to be toasted sits before the fire or over its coals, but never in its flames.

If you have an authentic fireplace toaster, the kind with a rack and feet, place it on the hearth in front of the fire to toast your bread. Antique examples of this implement are still fairly plentiful, but they do command high prices. Reproductions, which are generally cheaper and just as attractive as the originals, are a favorite commission of contemporary blacksmiths, since they give them a chance to display a variety of their skills.

Slices of bread, split muffins, and even bagels can also be toasted in the ordinary flat hinged grills sold for cooking hotdogs and hamburgers on your barbecue. These grills closely approximate the "double broilers" mentioned in *The Boston Cook Book of 1883*. They will hold about four slices of bread at one

Another way to broil your hot dogs, hamburgers, etc. is to place them in an ordinary two-sided barbecue grill with handles and prop before the fire. Again, foil is used to keep hearth clean and improve reflected heat.

time—at least twice the capacity of the wrought iron fireplace toasters and the toasting forks. The easiest way to toast bread slices in these grills is to prop them up before the fire with a log, pot, or brick at a fairly steep angle. When one side of the food is browned, turn the grill to toast the other side. These grills can also be held over a bed of coals to toast their contents, but this is more work for the cook.

Broiling in Early America

Unlike broiling in today's ovens, broiling on the American hearth was performed over the heat source—a bed of glowing coals—rather than under it— exactly the same technique that we use in our modern barbecue grills. But in contrast with the popularity barbecuing enjoys, broiling—or grilling, as it was sometimes called—was not a favored food preparation technique in early America. Fireplace cooks disliked the smoky flavor imparted to the food by the drippings of the cooking meat as they fell on the glowing coals. Also for broiled meat to be enjoyable, it had to be tender—a quality early American cooks were not accustomed to in their cuts of meat. The average housewife or cook had wild game or old, sinewy domestic animals as her source of meat. Neither was naturally tender, and broiling did nothing to improve this quality.

When meat was broiled at the early American hearth, the cook often parboiled it first. Parboiling ensured that the meat would be thoroughly cooked when it was removed from the grill, since broiling was described, and is in practice, a quick method of cooking foods. Parboiling chicken parts before broiling them was a common practice, and one that was recommended by Eliza Leslie. She observed that if one did not cook the thicker pieces of chicken, such as the thigh and leg, before broiling, they had a tendency to become charred on the outside while the inside remained raw.

The implements used for broiling food on the early American hearth were gridirons and broilers. The gridirons resembled square grills raised up from the hearth by short legs. A handle extended from one end. The cook placed these grills over a bed of coals to provide the heat necessary for broiling her food, and placed her meat directly on its well-greased bars. She let the underside of the steak (or other food) cook until done on this side and then poured any juices accumulated on its surface into a nearby dish and reserved them for later use. She then turned the food to cook its reverse side.

More elaborate gridirons were produced by some imaginative blacksmiths. These gridirons had slightly taller front legs and grooves or channels in the upper surfaces of the flat bars that made up the grilling area. As the meat cooked, its juices trickled down these grooves into a narrow trough at the lower end of the gridiron, and were poured off by the cook. These natural cooking juices were either served with the meat *au naturel*, as is, or were thickened to make a gravy.

Gridiron broiling on an antique (right) and on a new inexpensive reproduction from the Pottery Barn (left). Note coals are placed on foil to improve their heating ability and to keep the hearth clean and grease-free.

The other group of implements commonly used for broiling were themselves called broilers. The cooking area on these was usually round, and like the gridirons, they had a handle and short legs to raise the grilling area above a bed of coals. Many broilers had attractive wavy bars across their grilling surfaces instead of the ordinary straight ones standard on the gridiron. Apart from supporting the meat in style, and leaving attractive marks on the cooked food, this design variation had no apparent function. On some broilers, the circular grilling surface turned on its tripod-like legs, presumably allowing the cook to regulate the broiling temperature or to check her meat for doneness with ease. In another ingenious design, the broiler's bars had channels in them and were tilted slightly downward towards the center of the circular implement. As the meat cooked, its juices dripped down these channels, pooling into a central well, which then directed them still further into a handle, which doubled as a trough, and had a final, larger well in its end. Aside from these variations, the cook proceeded with her cooking on a broiler as she would have with a gridiron.

Techniques for Today: The Gridiron or Broiler and Fish Grill

Except for a few refinements, broiling is most easily performed in modern fireplaces in much the same way today as it was yesterday. The most important of these variations is to be sure to cover your hearth cooking area with several thicknesses of aluminum foil before you begin your broiling. This step will not only save you a messy clean-up job when your cooking is completed, but will prevent grease from accumulating on your hearth and causing a potentially hazardous fire.

The implements best suited for fireplace broiling today are antique gridirons and broilers, or copies of them, and the basket fish grills with feet on top and bottom, commonly sold in gourmet kitchen equipment stores for barbecue use. The Bridge Kitchenware Corporation, Inc., is an excellent source for these grills. They are listed in Chapter 10, Sources for Hearth Cookware and Accessories.

To broil in your fireplace, choose an area for cooking, if space permits, that is away from your central fire. Cover the hearth floor here with several thicknesses of heavy-duty aluminum foil, cutting the sheets slightly larger than the size of your broiling implement. Next season your meat, or prepare it as your recipe directs, and place it on the gridiron or broiler, or in the fish grill. It is helpful to lightly oil the cooking bars of your grilling implement first, to prevent the food from sticking to these surfaces as it cooks. Then, when the fire has developed a healthy supply of red hot coals, begin cooking. First shovel a

A good way to broil trout is in a basket fish grill made today for barbecue use. Placing foil on the hearth under the coals will keep the hearth grease-free and make clean-up easier. Other fish, as well as small steaks and lamb chops can also be cooked this way.

generous amount of the coals onto the foil, and spread them out so that they cover an area equal to the whole grilling area of your implement, or to the underside of your food. Place the gridiron, broiler, or fish grill over these coals and let the food cook on one side until done to your liking. Then, if the food is cooking on a gridiron or broiler, turn it with a meat fork. (Before you do this, pour off any accumulated surface juices into a side dish.) To turn the food cooking in a fish grill, simply turn the whole device over so that it is now resting on its top legs, instead of its bottom ones.

It should not be necessary to refresh the coals for broiling, as they usually give off enough heat for twenty to thirty minutes of cooking, an adequate length of time to broil most foods. If you find that you do need to add more coals to complete your cooking, the best way to do this is to remove the gridiron or other implement from the foil cooking area before refreshing the coals.

This will prevent any ashes that may be disturbed from getting onto your food.

If your fireplace is too small to permit broiling in a location other than over the central fire, just lay your cooking fire on layers of foil, and let it die down to a bed of glowing coals, then broil right there. To clean up your fireplace: after dinner, when the coals are cold, simply fold up the foil, coals and all, and discard the whole package.

While hamburgers, steaks, and lamb chops are favorite broiled fireplace fare, fish cooked over the coals is a special culinary treat. This is where fireplace broiling strikes its tastiest note. And, as a final tip on broiling in your fireplace, fish grills are very handy for broiling small filet steaks, and chicken parts, as well as fish.

Browning Off: The Salamander and Ember Tongs

Since broiling was accomplished in the fireplace by placing food over the coals, the practice of running a casserole or other food under the broiler as we do today to give its surface a lovely, golden brown crust or glaze, was not possible. Instead, to brown off the tops of her food, the early cook brought the heat of the fire over it. For this purpose she frequently used an implement known as a salamander (Hannah Glasse calls it an "iron for browning off" in

Browning off tops of foods can easily be accomplished by holding a hot coal near their cooked surfaces. Here ember tongs are used to grip the coal, but ordinary kitchen or barbecue tongs, provided they are metal, will work just as well.

"Browning off" with an iron peel which has been preheated in the glowing coals.

her book *The Art of Cookery Made Plain and Easy*, 1796.) A salamander consisted of a circular metal disk, about one inch thick, which was attached to a long handle. The cook buried the disc end of the salamander in the coals until it was red hot and then held it close to the top of a pie pastry or the surfaces of any other foods that she wished to finish with a golden brown color. The unusual name for the implement is derived from the mythical salamander, an animal which had the power to endure fire. If the cook did not own a salamander, she "browned off" her foods by passing red hot coals over them, grasping the coals with a pair of ember or pipe tongs.

Both of these methods of browning off are recommended to the modern fireplace cook, in addition to the following substitutions. In place of a salamander, an iron peel or ash shovel could be heated in the coals of the fire and held over the food. But since the spade end of peels and ash shovels are much thinner than that of the traditional salamander, it will not hold as much heat, or retain it for as long a period of time, as the salamander will. Or in lieu of either the antique salamander or peel, a *crème brûlée* iron, sold through gourmet equipment stores and catalogs, works on the same principle as the salamander. Normally used for caramelizing the sugar topping on your *crème brûlée*, the implement can be used at your fireplace for finishing your pie crusts and casseroles. And, if ember or pipe tongs are not available, ordinary fireplace or barbecue tongs will work just as well for manipulating the hot coals.

5

Boiling, Simmering, Steaming, and Related Techniques

Brimming kettles of fragrant soups and stews bubbling on the hearth are surely among the first images to flash to one's mind when thinking of fireplace cookery. And undoubtedly the English ancestry of this country's earliest settlers and the cuisine they brought with them—one which favored boiling and simmering foods—is largely responsible for these lingering impressions. But as one begins to examine life in early America it becomes quickly apparent how well adapted a simmering pot of food was to our ancestor's way of life, and why boiling and steaming foods have continued to thrive in our cooking.

In Early America

The first American homemakers had to have been the original harried housewives. Among the many duties for which the colonial homemaker was responsible, cooking was just another chore, and a minor one, at that. Her duties were endless, and even the most basic items had to be prepared or fabricated by hand. She oversaw the family vegetable garden, preserved food for winter, spun thread and wove it into cloth garments, and blankets, made soap and candles, and raised her children. And she did not even have the benefit of running water, plumbing, or the numerous other simple aids we now regard as necessities.

With this overwhelming workload, time was a very precious commodity, and ease and speed of food preparation became crucial. Putting whatever food was available (thin'ins from the garden, or a freshly caught rabbit) into a large pot with water, and placing it over the fire was a most expedient way to prepare lunch and dinner. Among the easiest ways to cook foods, boiling and simmering offered many other advantages for the household.

Of all the food preparation techniques, a simmering pot also required the least attention from the cook. The kettle's contents were first brought to a boil, and any foam carefully skimmed off as it rose to the surface. The pot was then covered and left to simmer slowly on the back of the hearth, for hours, and sometimes even for days, as in the preparation of samp porridge. An Indian goulash eaten by the settlers, this consisted of a combination of corn-meal, meat, and vegetables. Samp porridge was cooked for at least three days, and was considered done when the mixture was so thick it could be removed from the pot in a solid chunk!

With the exception of an occasional stir, or the addition of more water to keep the pot from boiling dry, the simmering kettle required no other attention from the cook. While one did have to remember to keep the fire going, length of cooking time was not a major concern for these simple meals. Experience taught housewives that the soup or stew always tasted better on the second day, after the flavors of the different ingredients had had a chance to "marry."

The combination of boiling and slow simmering was also needed to tender-ize the generally tough pieces of meat the cook had at her disposal. Meat, especially beef, in early America did not have the finely marbled, tender quali-ties we are so accustomed to today. Cattle were not raised for slaughter, and the practice of tenderizing meat by grinding or chopping it into hamburger and adding fat, did not become popular until the late nineteenth or early twentieth century. Instead, as we have seen, the fireplace cook depended on infrequently slaughtered domestic livestock or wild game for the meat in her meals, and both were notoriously tough!

In the earliest years of America's settlement, domestic animals were very costly and scarce, since they had to be imported from England and Europe. As a result, cows, chickens, goats, and sheep were primarily raised for their milk, eggs, and wool, or to pull the farmer's plow. A milk cow, for example, cost $1,400 in 1620. And although by 1700 its price had dropped to $250, it was still a very valuable possession, considering that most rural housewives spent, on the average, $20 a year for their flour, sugar, and all other household staples combined. So when these animals finally did reach the cooking pot, they had more than outlived their usefulness, and certainly their tenderness.

One frequently comes across recipes in old cookbooks specifically for preparing the meat of animals that were past their prime. One such recipe, entitled "Soup of Any Kind of Old Fowl, The only way in which they are eat-able," is found in identical versions in *The Virginia Housewife*, by Mrs. Mary Randolph, and in *The Frugal Colonial Housewife*, by Susannah Carter. A recipe you're not likely to come across in cookbooks today, it directs the reader to first "Put the fowls in a coop and feed them moderately for a fortnight;"

Wild game, the cook's most regular source of meat, was tough, too. Possum, squirrel, rabbit, deer, bear, and moose were some of the plentiful native creatures that were most often found in the cook's pot, and they, too, needed hours of slow simmering to make them edible.

Even for roasting, parboiling the meat first was a technique many cooks relied upon to ensure a tender roast. While many of the more sophisticated cooks of the period frowned on this practice, as they felt it diminished the flavor of the meat, which surely it did, the meat probably required it.

Neither could homemakers of the past also be particular about the cuts of meat they cooked. They were grateful for whatever their husband or son was lucky enough to snare or shoot on any day to fill their cookpot.

This rather unpredictable method of obtaining meat also made these cooks quite frugal. Not sure of when the next rabbit or wild turkey would be theirs, they were very conscious of waste, and when confronted with a whole animal (the usual situation) were challenged to prepare every part of it, from horns to hooves, in a tasty fashion. Again, boiling and slow simmering were the methods the cook utilized to transform the less tender and more unusual cuts of meat into palatable and often delicious meals.

Ironically today's emphasis on broiling and roasting, and the pressure for fast meal preparations, has practically eliminated the preparation of these tougher but very tasty parts of an animal's anatomy from our diet in favor of the more speedily-cooked and more reliably tender, but definitely less flavorful, portions.

Another factor which popularized boiling and slow simmering as a method of food preparation was the Colonial way of life. The hard-working, rural farm existence of many early American families discouraged them from eating meals together at set times, as we do today. Sundays and holidays were an exception to this practice, but on most days, farm chores came first, and family members were usually too busy even to sit in the household's sole chair when dining. When they finally did stop to eat, meals were often hastily consumed standing before the hearth or board (the common name for the improvised or crude table) whenever one felt hungry and had a spare moment. So an ever-ready pot of dinner was a convenience for the diner, as well as for the cook.

And lastly, the softened nature of boiled and simmered foods probably made them widely preferred because of the generally poor condition of early American teeth. Inadequate diet and lack of care took their toll on the teeth of our ancestors. Pregnancy was especially hard on the women's teeth, and the adage, "A tooth (lost) for every child," was particularly applicable then. Throughout the general population teeth were weakened and/or missing entirely, too. And although everyone has heard of George Washington's famous wooden dentures, it is unlikely that the poorer members of society, or even the middle class, could have afforded such luxuries. As a consequence, the population was not able to manage food that required strenuous biting or chewing. Meals boiled and simmered until the meat was reduced to rags were easy for them to digest with little or no effort.

In view of these myriad factors, it is easy to understand why the simmering cookpot became a permanent fixture on every hearth and why the all-purpose iron pot used to produce these boiled and simmered meals was considered the most basic fireplace cooking implement. Indeed, in the seventeenth century, it was not infrequently the only pot a homemaker owned.

Commonly called a cooking kettle, or today a gypsy kettle, the early pots used to produce these boiled meats were usually cast of iron. They were rounded in shape with three short stubby feet, and were produced in a variety of sizes from very small to enormous. Most had handles which were attached, while others only had small loops on each side from which an adjustable handle which looked like big calipers was hooked. The feet raised the bottom of the pot above the fireplace floor so coals could be placed under it for cooking purposes. They also gave it stability when it was simply sitting on the hearth floor or other flat surface for serving or storing. The handle was used, of course, for lifting or moving the pot, but most importantly for hanging it over the fire from the crane or lugpole, its usual cooking position.

While the simple iron kettle was most popular, the basic version was sometimes improved with an enamel lining. This lining made the pots easier to keep clean and permitted certain foods to be cooked in them without the iron interacting with their flavor or color. Few examples of the lined kettles have survived with their linings intact or in usable condition.

Other metals were also used to make the common boiling vessel. Some of the largest and most beautiful examples we have seen have been made of copper. These were used outdoors for rendering pork fat, boiling down maple syrup, washing clothes, or making apple butter. These copper pots were much lighter than their iron versions, and were also more attractive, but they were not designed with feet, probably because copper feet would not have supported the weight of the full kettle. Instead, the bottoms of copper pots were usually flat and only their handles were made of a sturdier metal, such as iron. In place of feet or a handle, some of the largest copper kettles sat in their own circular iron frames or tripods over the fire. These frequently had rounded bottoms, which made them resemble giant mixing bowls. Inside the home, the smaller copper pots were designed to either hang from the crane or to rest on trivets, their usual "cooking" positions.

Occasionally cooking kettles were made of brass and even silver. A reference to silver kettles is made by Hannah Glasse in her eighteenth-century cookbook, *The Art of Cookery Made Plain and Easy*.

In addition to the general category of cooking kettles, early American kitchens were frequently equipped with a smaller, rounded-bottom pot which served the same purpose as our modern saucepan. Called posnets or skillets, these cousins of the cook's kettle were made of cast or wrought iron and were designed to sit over the coals on their short spindly legs. They were used for stewing small amounts of food, for making sauces, and generally for the same cooking needs as the large cook's kettle. Posnets, however, were called into play when smaller amounts of food were to be prepared.

In the seventeenth and eighteenth centuries, the dinner or luncheon meals prepared in these pots were broadly referred to as pottage. Roughly a cross between a soup and a stew, pottage was made from literally anything on hand. Vegetables, herbs, seasoning, and meat were all cut into small pieces and tossed into the cook's kettle with enough water to cover the ingredients. Generally assembled first thing in the morning, the combination was left to simmer slowly until mealtime.

In times of plenty, marvelous new recipes might result from the marriage of the unfamiliar native foods the settlers learned to enjoy, such as corn, and the usual combinations and substitutions of their own cooking heritages. All-American favorites, many of which were originally based on Indian dishes, such as Brunswick stew, clam chowder, and succotash, evolved this way.

Even under less bountiful circumstances, the kettle could produce surprisingly delicious results. Philadelphia pepper pot, a truly original American recipe, resulted from this imaginative "cook-what-you-have" approach. The soup was the inspiration of General George Washington's chef. The story is told that George Washington asked his camp cook to fix a special dinner to raise the morale of his haggard and hungry troops. The chef, undaunted by the limited supplies in his larder—tripe and generous supply of peppercorns—cooked them together in the kettle with water and produced a wonderful soup which all enjoyed and which they named in honor of the chef's inventiveness, after the city of his birth.

In winter, especially during its latter months, pottage could be as meager as flour soup, made from only milk and browned flour—a dish probably most commonly served during the last months of winter, from March until the first spring growth appeared, when food supplies were at their lowest. The colonists called this period "starving time," since it was reminiscent of the first winters of colonization when many did die of starvation.

Breakfast porridge was also a common food prepared in the big iron pot. Often mixed after the supper meal had emptied the contents of the pot, the porridge was left in the waning embers of the fire to cook slowly overnight in readiness for the next morning's meal. Porridge could also be cooked or reheated for several days, as in the Mother Goose rhyme: "Pease-porridge in the pot, nine days old."

Another product of the kettle was pocket or portable soup, our forefathers' version of the bouillon cube. Pocket soup came yesterday, as it does today, in two flavors: brown, beef-based; and white, chicken-based. The preparation of each was similar and required a lengthy and complicated reduction of the meat (which determined its color and flavor), vegetables, and water. Salt was omitted and added later when the cubes were reconstituted in water to use as a soup base, or to enrich sauces. An especially detailed and excellent description of how the early American housewife made these "soup concentrates" is given in *The Frugal Colonial Housewife* by Susannah Carter.

Pocket soup was frequently carried on long trips by travelers and hunters, since it was so readily portable in one's pocket—hence its name. They would either let a cube of this soup melt in their mouths for nourishment when on the go, or, when time permitted, would drop one in boiling water at their campsite. With the addition of dried beans or corn, it made a very satisfying meal.

And, last but not least, the kettle was famous for its boiled dumplings and puddings. They came in great variety, and among them was the still familiar Indian and festive plum puddings, as well as an exotic pigeon pudding. While they haven't survived the swings in taste and current style in cuisine as well as soups and stews, boiled puddings were immensely popular and a staple of the early American diet.

The general procedure for their preparation was to wrap the pudding or dumpling mixture (a typical recipe called for fruit, eggs, flour, milk, and spices) in a thick pudding cloth that was first scalded in boiling water and then dredged in flour. To facilitate its filling and tying, the cloth was placed in a deep bowl so its sides could be easily drawn up around the soft mixture. The cloth was then filled and tied firmly, with plenty of room allowed for the pudding to swell as it cooked. The tying place was pasted with a small lump of moistened flour, an extra measure to keep the boiling water out. To quote Eliza Leslie, "If any water gets into the pudding it will be spoiled."

The pudding package was then lowered into a kettle filled with boiling water. A lid was placed on the pot, and it was left to cook for anywhere from two hours for a smallish meat dumpling to six for a large plum pudding. The pudding or dumpling was turned occasionally as it boiled to ensure even cooking.

Sometimes, instead of immersing her puddings in boiling water, the cook suspended them in the steam over a pot of soup to cook. Cooked by this method they could be more accurately called "steamed" rather than "boiled" puddings. Another variation was to place the pudding mixture in a simple metal can or a decorative pottery mold, if the cook was lucky enough to own one. These containers gave the cooked pudding a more attractive appearance than the free-form shape which resulted from the use of the pudding cloth.

Cooks were careful to keep the water in which the pudding cooked boiling at all times, and to replenish the pot, as it boiled away, with boiling water only. The introduction of cold water would have slowed down the cooking action in the pot and caused the finished pudding to be hard and heavy. A filled, hot teakettle was kept on the hearth for this purpose.

Puddings were served hot, and were not removed from the cooking pot until moments before they were to be served. Their generally bland flavor was usually enhanced at the table with a wine or cream sauce or a simple topping of sugar (or molasses), butter, and cinnamon. Leftover pudding was served the next day, sliced and fried.

Puddings and dumplings can be prepared much in the same manner today as they were yesterday. And while the cloth bag method just described can be copied with a fair amount of success, a modification of this technique that we feel is easier and produces results more in keeping with contemporary tastes is given in the Techniques for Today section of this chapter, which follows.

The kettle was also capable of cooking two foods at once, a real energy-and time-saver, especially if you only had one pot! To accomplish this, the pudding was either cooked in the steam over a soup or other hot kettle, as described earlier in this chapter, or, if the cook was in a hurry to speed up the cooking process, she lowered the pudding right into the kettle's contents. Cooks who practiced this last technique claimed that the foods did not exchange flavors as they cooked together—or perhaps, if they did, it didn't bother them. This is a remarkable claim which we haven't verified in our fireplace cooking sessions! But an interesting observation on this unusual cooking practice has been suggested by Waverly Root and Richard de Rochemont in their excellent book, *Eating In America, A History*, published by William Morrow and Company. They propose that these mixed-food cooking habits have been in part responsible for Americans being unable to recognize fine shadings of taste, a failing we are frequently accused of today.

Beginning in the mid-eighteenth century, foods prepared in the all-purpose American cook-pot became much more sophisticated. Instead of just cutting meat into small pieces and tossing it into the kettle with whatever else was available, more attention was given to the final appearance and texture of the boiled dinners. A practice known as collaring, in which a joint was boned, rolled, and tied, became popular. Collaring meat prevented it from losing its shape or from falling apart in the lengthy boiling process. As a result, the boiled dinner could be neatly sliced after it was cooked and attractively presented at the table. Vegetables were still added to the boiling pot, but not until the meat was nearing completion, so that they would not become overcooked. Distinctions were also made between soups, stews, and ragouts. And one-dish meals were no longer referred to as pottage.

Recipes in early cookbooks that specified boiling and its related techniques—simmering, steaming, poaching, braising, and stewing—were plentiful, varied, and interesting. And directions for preparing almost every category of food, from puddings and breads to meat, fish, fowl, and vegetables, using one of these techniques, were included in all the early recipe collections. This is an indication of how much more popular boiling and its related techniques were yesterday than they are today.

In 1770, Martha Bradley summarized the principle of boiling food rather succinctly for her readers, we feel. "Boiling," she wrote, "is the Dressing (of) Things by means of Water, as Roasting does it by the naked Fire…"

And Amelia Simmons offered the following rules to be observed when cooking food in this manner:

> The First necessary caution is that your pots and covers are always kept clean—be careful that your pot is constantly boiling, by this means you may determine with precision the time necessary to accomplish any dish you may wish to prepare in this way. Put fresh meat into boiling water, and salt into cold. Never crowd your pot with meat, but leave sufficient room for plenty of water. Allow a quarter of an hour to every pound of meat.

While these directions from the past for boiling may seem curious, this method of cooking food, and its related techniques—simmering, steaming, poaching, and braising—are still performed in much the same way today as they were yesterday. With a few modifications on the procedures used by the early American housewife, here is how to accomplish these techniques in your fireplace.

Techniques for Today

To boil, simmer, steam, braise, and poach, or in general to "dress food with water" in your fireplace, your most important implement will be a rather generous-sized pot with a lid. While we acknowledge that all these simple techniques can be executed in almost any size and shape vessel that is fireproof and holds water (some American Indians used freshly killed buffalo stomachs for this purpose), the large iron cook's kettle of yesterday was, and still is, the best implement for performing these tasks at the kitchen hearth.

The Cook's Kettle or Gypsy Kettle, and the Posnet

The original iron cook's kettle described earlier in this chapter is well suited to all of these cooking techniques, since it was intended expressly for these uses in a fireplace. When cooking, the kettle either hangs over the fire securely from an S hook on the crane, or from an adjustable trammel anchored in the chimney throat, or it rests comfortably over coals on the hearth. In addition, an antique kettle, which will lend an authentic air to your cooking activities, can most likely be found for a fairly reasonable price at a local antique shop, or even at a flea market. They were plentifully produced and were virtually indestructible, so many of them have survived undisturbed to this day. If you prefer a new kettle, good reproductions of the original cook's kettle are also being cast today.

The only drawback to the traditional cook's kettle is that it was not originally designed and produced with its own lid. If some kettles did come outfitted with lids, this piece has long since disappeared. And for many of the following cooking techniques, especially steaming, a closely fitting lid is most desirable. This accessory is also generally handy for keeping straying embers and ashes out of the soup or to step up the heating process. To improvise or make a new lid for an old cooking pot, either borrow a lid from one of your kitchen pots or make a new one out of wood. Wooden lids are commonly in use with iron kettles of antique design at Plimoth Plantation. A word of precaution when using a lid from another pot: We have found that if the lid fits too snugly, there is a tendency for it to be sucked into the pot as the old iron expands from exposure to the fire's heat, causing a loud explosive sound and spattering the contents of the kettle. Selecting a lid that is slightly larger than seems necessary will avoid this problem, as will the use of a wooden lid, since the wood will expand from contact with the rising steam from the kettle, precluding the possibility of its falling into the soup.

The most common cooking position of these kettles, and the most versatile, is suspended over the fire from a crane by an S hook. To adjust the temperature of the kettle on the crane, the cook has three basic options. First she can slide the S hook holding the kettle along the crane, which will place the pot further away from or closer to the fire. Second, she can use a shorter or longer pothook to raise or lower the kettle. And third, she can swing the crane like a gate to almost any location in front of the fire and even out into the room. This last position is recommended for filling the pot, skimming its surface, testing or sampling the food in it, or serving its contents, since it is safest and easiest for the cook, and doesn't require that she lean over the hot fire to reach the kettle.

If your fireplace is not equipped with a crane, the second-best way of heating the kettle is to hang it over the fire from an adjustable trammel hung in the chimney throat. A trammel does not offer as many possibilities as does the crane for controlling the cooking temperature or the position of the pot, but this device does allow the cook to raise or lower her pot over the fire.

Yet another alternative for heating the kettle is to place it on the hearth near the fire and to shovel a generous amount of coals under it. This last option is a great deal of work, requiring a plentiful supply of coals, frequent fire-tending, and almost constant surveillance of the pot by the cook to maintain a steady cooking temperature.

Having just outlined the basics of the use of the kettle with the cooking fire, we will describe how to execute the techniques of boiling, simmering, braising, steaming, and poaching in it at your hearth.

To boil in the kettle, it must be placed in the hottest position, or directly (about six to eight inches) above the flames of a small, but brisk and well-established fire. Boiling, as all cooks know, is characterized by lots of steam rising from the pot and large bubbles rapidly breaking the surface of the liquid. This action causes a walloping motion, which early American cooks used as a temperature measurement when cooking. They counted the frequency of the wallops to get an indication of how hot the liquid was, and therefore how long to cook the food immersed in it.

After a time, depending on the fire's intensity, the proximity of your pot to it, and the amount of food and liquid in your pot, its contents will reach a boil. There is a common saying that "a watched pot never boils," but the use of a lid will help matters along considerably.

Simmering, which is directly related to boiling, is cooking liquids at a temperature just below the boiling point. This temperature is reached when many tiny bubbles rise to the surface of the pot. Simmering obviously requires less heat than boiling, but it is accomplished in the same way. To simmer foods, place the kettle in the hottest position at your hearth—or on the crane directly over the fire—and cover it with a lid. When the liquid reaches the simmering point, maintain this temperature by moving the pot further away from the fire, either by sliding the S hook along the crane, swinging the crane further away from the fire, adjusting the trammel, or in any of the other ways outlined earlier of moving the pot away from the fire and thus adjusting its temperature.

While these are basically foolproof and self-explanatory techniques, a few specific rules governing boiling and simmering foods, which early American cooks adhered to and which still hold true today, follow.

When one is preparing a broth or stock, the meat and vegetables should be put into a cold pot with cold water and the ingredients slowly heated together. When the meat is to be the end product, it should be added to the pot after the water has reached the boiling point. And, as Eliza Leslie observed, "...if the fire is too great, and the soup boils too fast, the meat will become hard and tough, and will not give off its juices."

To boil a twenty-first-century pudding in the cook's kettle, use an empty one-pound coffee can as a mold and grease the inside. Place your pudding mixture or other recipe batter in the can. Some breads can also be prepared in this manner. An example is the brown bread recipe in Chapter 7. The uncooked ingredients should only fill one-half to two-thirds of the can, in order to allow for expansion. Cover the can with a double thickness of waxed paper or aluminum foil, and secure the cover with string. Place the can (covered end up) on a trivet or rack in a large kettle and fill with enough boiling water to come halfway up the sides of the mold. Cover the kettle and boil until the pudding is done.

The kettle should be checked occasionally as the cooking proceeds and more boiling water should be added, if needed, to maintain the original water level. Add only boiling water to the kettle! (A teakettle on the hearth is a good, constant, source for hot water.) After the cooking is completed, the pudding should be removed from the can while still hot, sliced, and served warm, traditionally with a sauce or other topping.

Another less frequently used but nonetheless interesting technique, related to "dressing food with water," and which can also be performed in the cook's kettle, is braising. Braising is the cooking of foods in a small amount of liquid, such as broth, wine, or water. To braise food in the kettle, first preheat the empty pot by hanging it over the fire—from the crane is best. Then sear your chicken or other meat in it in a small amount of butter or oil. Carefully rotate the food as it browns, being careful not to pierce its surface or skin, thus releasing its juices. After the meat is nicely colored on all sides, add a small amount of the braising liquid to the pot, together with herbs, seasonings, vegetables, or whatever ingredients your specific recipe calls for. Cover the pot and lower the cooking temperature by sliding the kettle along the crane away from the fire, by swinging the crane forward, or by any other appropriate means of temperature adjustment. Continue cooking at this lower temperature until the food is done, adding more of the braising liquid to the pot if it should become dry.

Steaming is another easy technique which is at home in the versatile kettle. To steam foods in it, place the pot in the hottest position on the hearth—suspended over the fire from the crane is again best—and fill it a quarter of the way up from the bottom with water. Cover and bring the water to a boil, and then place the food to be cooked in a basket or on a rack, inside the kettle, and support it in the steam over the hot water to cook. Steam the food until done, adding additional boiling water as needed to complete the cooking. Be sure to add only boiling water to the kettle, as the introduction of cold or even warm water could stop, or reduce, the steaming action and ruin your dish. Again, a teakettle is handy as a supply of boiling water at your hearth.

Poaching foods (eggs and fish are commonly associated with this technique) is another method of cooking food in water that lends itself readily to the cook's kettle. Although specially designed fish-poachers with handles for hanging them from a crane over the fire graced a few of the better-equipped and wealthier early American hearths, the all-purpose cooking kettle was again the implement most often used for this procedure. In poaching, food is gently cooked in a barely simmering liquid such as water, wine, or *court bouillon* on a flat strainer or pierced tray which permits easy removal and draining of the food when it is done.

To poach eggs in the cook's kettle, one can use the individual metal egg-poachers found in hardware stores. If you don't have these, vigorously stir the hot poaching water until it swirls around the sides of the pot. Then gently ease in a raw egg by slipping it out of its shell into the swirling water's vortex. The circular action of the hot water will "poach" the egg while preserving its round shape.

To poach larger foods, such as a fish, place a small circular rack outfitted with two large hooks at either edge (hooks can be improvised from coat-hanger wire) in the bottom of the kettle. These hooks will serve as handles for lifting out the fish and draining off the cooking liquid. Place the fish on your rack and cover the pot, poaching until done. And don't despair if your fish is larger than the diameter of your cooking pot. This is a common problem and can be remedied by tucking the fish's tail in its mouth so that is conforms to the circular shape of the kettle, a trick early American cooks frequently relied upon.

To perform many of the above cooking tasks with a small amount of food, the contemporary chef, as did her early American counterpart, will find the posnet a useful alternative to the large cook's kettle. If you are fortunate enough to own an antique example of this cooking implement or even a reproduction, how it is used in a fireplace will be obvious in its design. The posnet sits on the hearth over a small pile of hot coals, raked or shoveled forward from your central cooking fire. Its short legs and regular pot handle are perfectly designed for this application. Proceed with your cooking, refreshing the coals underneath the pot as needed to maintain a steady cooking temperature. Adding more coals will raise the cooking temperature, removing coals will lower it. If you don't happen to have a posnet in your inventory, any ordinary kitchen saucepan, placed on a trivet to raise it above the coals, is a simple and satisfactory substitute.

A special teakettle with a "tilter" (pictured) is a rare commodity, but simplifies pouring tea from a heavy, hot pot over the fire. A "tilter" pot hook which a blacksmith can easily make for you will adapt any ordinary kettle to fireplace use and will also permit the cook to tip her kettle without removing it.

The Teakettle

Before we finish this chapter, we feel we can't omit at least a passing mention of another boiling device, the teakettle. Nothing is more pleasing on a brisk winter's day than a hot cup of tea, and a teakettle also is a hospitable sight in your fireplace.

Eighteenth-century Americans doted on their afternoon tea, in part because of the customs of their English ancestry and also because of their poorly heated homes. And until the infamous tax on tea made it unpopular and unpatriotic, afternoon tea was a widespread ritual and a time for the ladies to socialize, gossip, and take a breather from the day's activities—the original coffee break. Elaborate china tea sets and silver tea balls and strainers, many of which now exist solely in museums, were some of the attendant accessories used to prepare and serve tea in early America, where they were among the most highly prized possessions owned by a housewife.

Early teakettles for heating water for tea, and for other cooking purposes in the fireplace, were usually cast of iron and were oversized affairs when compared with today's models. They were very heavy and generally were hung from the crane on an S hook. Some of these early teakettles had three small feet, which allowed the cook to sit the kettle on the hearth. Occasionally these iron kettles displayed innovative tilters, devices which permitted the cook to pour water from the heavy, hot kettle without requiring her to lift it off the crane. Tilters consisted of long, stationary lever-like handles attached to the kettle body between its spout and lid. To pour hot water from the kettle, the cook simply pushed down on the tilter, which tipped the kettle's spout downward, emptying its contents into a waiting cup.

Also developed for use with the teakettle were separate tilters. These were really modified pothooks which hung from the crane. They worked on the same leverage principle as the attached tilters, but their advantage was that they transformed any ordinary teakettle into one from which the cook could pour hot water without removing it from the crane.

In wealthier homes, probably the heavy duty iron teakettles were relegated to use in the kitchen fireplaces. In these households, most likely, the lighter-weight kettles made of the more expensive and attractive metals, such as copper and brass, were brought to the dining room and tea tables. These fancier teakettles are often pictured warming before the fire on fancy, tall trivets called footmen.

Old teakettles are rare and sought-after antiques. The most scarce and expensive are those with attached tilters, but even the separate tilter-pothook accessories are very rare. Still one can readily have a reproduction tilter or a double-pronged pothook (to give it more stability) fabricated to suspend your twentieth-century kitchen teakettle over the fire. And if you don't have a crane in your fireplace, a trivet will complete a modern pot's transition from cooktop to hearth.

6

Frying and Sautéing

In Early America

While Southern cooks were famous for their ability to prepare an entire—and delicious—meal in a frying pan, fried foods did not enjoy this same degree of popularity with fireplace cooks throughout America. Deep-fat frying over live coals, near an open fire, was inherently too dangerous. Wooden cooking utensils, spoons, and spatulas threatened to catch fire when they came in contact with the nearly boiling hot oil. And the hot fat could easily spatter, or the frying pan could tip, spilling its contents, and seriously burning the cook or an unwary child. Such accidents could also cause disastrous fires. A fire each week was recorded during the first winter in Boston, and at Plimoth Plantation, one winter, seven of its thirty-two buildings burned to the ground. Frying food was also in need of constant surveillance to ensure that it cooked properly. The earliest fireplace cooks were not willing or able to lavish such serious attention on their cooking activities, since complicated meal preparation usually meant that some other pressing chore would be shortchanged or ignored. Fried food was also not stylish. Mrs. Bradley described frying as "...a coarse and greasy Kind of Cookery, in Fashion in the Country, where there are great Appetites, and strong Stomachs, but is at present entirely left off in genteel Families..."

Despite these drawbacks, a number of delicious foods were prepared by frying them at the hearth. Among these delicacies the most famous recipe was for chicken dredged in flour or dipped in batter and then fried in oil—our now popular Southern fried chicken. It was introduced by the well-known Southern cook, Mrs. Randolph. Other foods frequently fried were small fish and oysters. But beef and other meats were usually thinly sliced into steaks and sautéed rather than deep-fat fried.

Toasts for garnishing dishes, fritters and doughnuts of infinite variety, and hush puppies were also commonly cooked in hot fat by fireplace chefs. Hush puppies were a cornmeal-based batter bread that were cooked by dropping spoonfuls of the mixture into hot fat. It was a favorite dish of hunters, since it was easily prepared at their campfires, and it is from them that this food derived its name. As the hush puppies cooked, their tantalizing aroma made the hunters' hungry dogs howl in eager anticipation of dinner. To quiet them, the hunter often tossed a piece of the bread to his hounds, admonishing them, "Hush, puppies."

Eggs were also fried by fireplace cooks. In addition to the more usual preparation of sautéing scrambled eggs, omelets, or "sunnyside up" eggs, in a small amount of butter, early cooks also fried raw eggs into a round ball by breaking them into the vortex of very hot swirling fat. These deep-fried eggs were generally used as a garnish for other dishes, rather than as a breakfast or supper entrée.

Less frequently fried or sautéed by early American cooks were vegetables. But some avant garde cookbooks of the day departed from the norm and recommended, instead of the usual boiling, sautéing of sliced potatoes. These potatoes were the first home fries consumed at the American table. Eggplant

Large, long-handled frying pans were often used in early American kitchens. Their exceptional handles kept the cook at a comfortable distance from the fire's heat and her long skirts safely away from its flame. These pans were usually placed on special trivets with a bracket which held their handle up. Coals were placed under the pan to cook the food.

was another vegetable that fireplace cooks were encouraged to fry. An early recipe for fried eggplant directed that it be cut into strips and breaded before it was immersed in the hot fat.

For deep-fat frying and sautéing, the fireplace cook had a number of implements at her disposal. Among them was a large, long-handled frying pan. And its handle was long—often extending to as much as three feet or more. These handles permitted the cook to fry her food while she remained standing, and kept her long skirts at a safe distance from the treacherous hot fat in the pan. These frying pans were placed on trivets with generous amounts of coals under them to provide the heat necessary for these cooking activities. Sometimes the

Doughnut kettle for frying doughnuts and fritters is suspended from the crane on a two pronged pothook to give it extra stability.

supporting trivets had a sliding bracket, or rest, to balance the extraordinary long handles of these pans. The rest could support the handle independently, thereby freeing the cook to move closer to inspect or turn her frying food, or to attend to other tasks nearby. But even with this special aid, a frying pan on a trivet was a precarious arrangement at best, and one that was liable to tip over at the slightest provocation.

A more stable design for frying vessels was incorporated in the frying pans that stood over the coals on their own three legs. These pans were affectionately called "spiders" by the early American housewife. Their spindly legs, emanating from the blackened round frying pan, made them resemble overgrown spiders. Spiders came in various sizes and heights, and were much safer for fireplace frying than the large frying pans. In addition to the extra stability afforded by their attached legs, their heavier weight (they were usually cast of iron) made them less likely to be knocked over accidentally.

Two other implements widely used for frying and sautéing by the fireplace cook were the doughnut kettle and the hanging griddle. Doughnut kettles were shallow, cast iron pots with a bail by which the cook hung them from her crane. A double-pronged pothook was probably used for hanging these pots, since a single S hook would have not provided enough stability for this wide, shallow pan to permit safe frying. The hanging griddle, discussed earlier in Chapter 3, Baking, was also used for frying in a small amount of oil, the technique we know as sautéing. Potatoes, scrambled eggs, and French toast were just a few of the foods that could be "fried" or sautéed on this implement.

The common medium for frying foods used by the early American cook was either hog's lard or beef drippings. Butter and olive oil (also known as sweet oil) were just too expensive, though for sautéing, which used a smaller quantity of fat, butter was sometimes used, as it improved the flavor of the final product. When frying, Mrs. Bradley mentioned that the pan should be clean and the fire brisk. "...Smoak will get in if there be any." Other early cookbook authors also recommended that the frying oil be brought to the boiling point before the food was put into it. The food should fry quickly, they specified, but not allowed to become too dark. Eliza Leslie advised frying small fish, such as flounder and perch, five minutes on each side, in hot lard that covered them completely. She also suggested a unique way of testing the temperature of the oil for frying. "You may know when the lard or dripping is hot enough, by dipping in the tail of one of the fish. If it becomes crisp immediately, the lard is in a proper state for frying." When the food was cooked to the desired degree of doneness, it was removed from the hot oil with a regular spatula or a modified version with drainage holes, called a fish slice, and placed on a coarse towel to absorb the excess fat before serving.

Techniques for Today

Although today's modern kitchens have vastly improved the safety of frying, and perhaps made it a more popular method of food preparation than it was, it still remains as dangerous a technique to perform in one's fireplace today as it was 150 years ago. For this reason, we can't honestly recommend deep-fat frying at the open hearth to our readers. It's just too risky. But since any general discussion of food preparation and cooking techniques would be incomplete without mentioning it, and its safer sister, sautéing, we have included our observations on how to most safely and easily execute these two techniques in your fireplace.

Deep-Fat Frying: The Spider and the Dutch Oven

If you must deep-fat fry in your fireplace, the safest two implements at your disposal are an antique spider and your Dutch oven. Both implements are most stable on the hearth floor. And in fact, some books on cooking with cast iron implements even recommend that the first time you cook in a new Dutch oven you fry in it, as this is an easy and reliable way of seasoning its new surfaces. Both spider and Dutch oven will permit deep-fat frying, but of the two we slightly prefer the Dutch oven. The average Dutch oven will, in general, hold more oil than most spiders. Its straight, deep sides can in some instances accommodate a frying basket. It comes already equipped with a lid, which you may need to ensure thorough cooking of thicker pieces of food, such as chicken. And reproduction Dutch ovens are readily available, while antique spiders are fairly uncommon, and new ones are not being mass-produced, to our knowledge.

To fry your food in either of these implements, place them over a healthy bed of coals and add enough vegetable oil or shortening to reach the level necessary for frying your food. Do not fill the pan to its edge, but leave enough room for the displacement caused by the addition of the food to be fried, and for the bubbling and rolling motion caused by the oil as it cooks the food. Let the oil preheat over the coals and test its readiness for frying with a piece of bread. Frying oil should be hot enough so that a cube of dry bread, dropped into it, becomes golden brown in about a minute's time. Delicate wisps of smoke will rise from the surface of the oil at this temperature. If the whole surface of the pot is smoking, the oil is too hot.

To begin frying, gently ease your batter-dipped or floured food into the hot fat one or two pieces at a time with a metal spatula or tongs. Do not crowd them, or add too many at once, as this will lower the temperature of the oil and your food will not turn out as crisp and light as it should. Remove the pieces as they are cooked and drain on paper toweling placed on the shelf of a reflector bake oven or on a cookie sheet. Place cooked food near the fire to keep it warm while you fry the remaining food. When you are frying thicker foods, such as chicken parts, it also may be necessary to place a lid on the frying pot to ensure the food is thoroughly cooked when the outside crust appears browned.

Fresh coals may have to be shoveled under the spider or Dutch oven in order to maintain an adequate temperature for frying successive batches of food. To do this, carefully push the fresh embers under the spider or the Dutch oven with a fireplace shovel. Do this with extreme caution so as not to get any embers into the hot oil, or to knock over the frying vessel. Never, under any circumstances, should you lift the spider or Dutch oven when it is filled with hot oil—this despite the fact that lifting the cooking pot is the standard, and generally easiest, method of replenishing coals under the Dutch oven, and is advised in the baking chapter and elsewhere in this book. Nor should you ever consider deep-fat frying in a pot suspended from the crane, such as in an antique doughnut kettle you may own, as the potential for the hot fat to tip over on the cook or into the fire is too great.

Sautéing: The Spider and the Hanging Griddle

Now that we have thoroughly discouraged you from deep-fat frying in your fireplace, we would like to discuss the ease and merits of an alternative method of frying at your hearth, sautéing. Many implements lend themselves readily to sautéing, the cooking of food in a small amount of fat. Among these, especially useful for fireplace sautéing is the spider, the long-handled antique frying pan (or even a modern short-handled one for that matter) placed on a trivet, and the hanging griddle.

Sautéing in a small spider.

Sautéing on, or in, any of these three implements is a simple process, much the same from one utensil to another. First, a small amount of oil or butter, or a combination of the two, should be applied to their slightly preheated surfaces. Mixing the oil with the butter will increase the temperature to which the butter can be heated before it burns—a useful trick if it takes a long time to cook your food. Place the food to be sautéed in the hot fat and let it cook until done on one side. Turn food with a metal spatula or tongs and continue cooking on the other side. Remove the food and serve. Or, if you wish, keep it warm while you prepare a sauce to serve with it. To do this, deglaze the sautéing pan by adding a small amount of wine or other liquid, such as chicken broth, to the fats and juices left in it. Cook slightly, stirring with a whisk until sauce is slightly reduced in quantity and thickened. (This last step will not be possible on the griddle.)

To provide the heat necessary for sautéing, frying pans and spiders rely on a supply of hot coals placed under their frying surfaces. And even the hanging griddle, which is usually hung on the crane by the cook, could be used for sautéing on the hearth floor too, if it is a footed model, with legs tall enough to permit placing a layer of coals under it. A footless hanging griddle can be placed on a trivet to adapt it to hearth sautéing, too. And in sautéing, unlike deep-fat frying, these pans can usually be lifted safely if it becomes necessary to replenish their cooking coals.

Sautéing can also be done on a hanging griddle, provided only a small amount of fat is needed. Here French toast is being browned in butter.

7

Fireplace Receipts for Hearth Cooking

Now that we have outlined in theory how to perform all the basic cooking techniques in a fireplace, here are some recipes you can use to put these new skills into practice. We have cooked and enjoyed many foods in our fireplaces, and the following collection represents a sampling of these, chosen to illustrate the use of every implement and cooking technique discussed in the book. All the fireplace implements and cooking techniques discussed in preceding chapters are utilized at least once, and some, because of their reliability, ease of use, and versatility (notably the Dutch oven), are mentioned more frequently.

These recipes were written expressly for open-hearth cooking, and some of the directions are noticeably unlike anything encountered in any other contemporary cookbook. So here are a few guidelines on how to interpret and use them.

Before you begin mixing up ingredients for a dish, we recommend that you read the recipe all the way through. It may be necessary to refresh your memory by referring to earlier accounts of the procedure for using an implement or executing a fireplace cooking technique required by the recipe, since in the interest of saving time and avoiding repetition, we have not repeated in each recipe every last step and fine point of each implement's use, or the details of executing specific fireplace techniques. To review this information in its entirety, refer back to the Techniques for Today sections of the appropriate chapters.

The recipes are arranged as follows: The ingredients are listed first, in the order in which they are used, with substitutions noted. Unless otherwise specified, eggs are large, and flour all-purpose. Next comes the preparation of the ingredients—cutting, dicing, sifting, peeling, etc.—and their method of mixing and cooking. After this comes the food's test for doneness and the approxiimate number of people the recipe serves. Included in each recipe and its general method are remarks on the fireplace equipment, heat, and cooking time, and, finally tips on successfully and easily preparing and serving each particular food at the hearth.

Under hearth cookware, the implement of choice is listed first. If you don't happen to have this item in your inventory, other pots or improvised equivalents are listed next. These will allow you to cook the food in your fireplace with the same results as you would achieve with the early American vessel or cooking tool. In some cases no satisfactory alternative utensil exists. In those cases, you may have to wait to try the recipe.

Under fire, general cooking temperatures or ranges are given. For more information on using and controlling the heat of the fire with the implement or technique specified, again refer back to the Techniques for Today sections in the appropriate chapters to find a detailed description of the regulation of the fire's heat for that procedure.

Approximate cooking times are also given. While these are fairly accurate, be sure to test the food for doneness before serving. Meat thermometers and cake testers are essential for thicker roasts and cakes.

A few of the more complicated recipes direct you to mix or do preliminary cooking of ingredients in your kitchen, and to do only the final cooking of the food at the fireplace. This is for the chef's convenience in certain recipes; but it is a suggestion that may well be utilized in many other recipes, too, since most fireplaces used for cooking today are not in or near your kitchen where all your spices, mixing bowls, baking pans, etc., are stored and handy.

Here, then, are the recipes. A quick glance will reveal that they have a homey American farm house bent. Please do not limit your fireplace cooking horizons solely to early American dishes, which were primarily English fare. We are perfectly comfortable roasting a duck, Chinese style, in our tin kitchen, or baking Italian pizza in our Dutch oven as we are boiling a plum pudding in our gypsy kettle.

For the purist, an abundance of excellent cookbooks covering American recipes and menus can be found on the shelves of most public libraries. A number of these books were especially helpful to us in our research, and we have identified them for your convenience in the bibliography at the back of this book. Remember, when adapting recipes from any other source for fireplace cooking, that it may take slightly longer to cook food in your fireplace than it does with a modern appliance. Also refer to the table on page 155 for adapting old recipes to contemporary weights and measures.

Starters, Soups, and Warming Libations

Roasted Grapefruit

Citrus fruits, such as grapefruits, were considered luxury foods in early America and served in only the wealthiest of homes. Other more commonly found orchard fruits can be roasted too such as pears, apples, and peaches. Roasting brings out the natural sweetness of these fruits trending them towards dessert, rather than meal openers.

Grapefruit halves can also be wrapped in foil and baked Indian-style in the hot coals. After they're heated through, open the foil and proceed to brown off tops following the recipe directions.

3 large grapefruits	6 tablespoons honey

Cut grapefruits in half. Loosen sections from membrane and skin with a small serrated knife. Top each half with 1 tablespoon of honey. Place on a hanging griddle suspended from a crane over a hot fire. When the grapefruit is warm, glaze tops by holding a red hot coal (with tongs) over the honey coating for a few moments.

SERVES: 6

HEARTH COOKWARE: hanging griddle (make do: reflector bake oven, pan on a trivet), ember tongs (make do: metal kitchen or barbeque tongs)

FIRE: hot with coals

Spider Corn Oysters

Serve these fireside, hot from the spider with soy sauce or a sprinkling of sugar. Fresh or frozen corn kernels can also be used.

One 11-ounce can corn niblets, drained
1 egg, slightly beaten
½ cup flour
½ teaspoon salt

⅛ teaspoon freshly ground black pepper
½ cup diced scallions
4 tablespoons oil (or more if needed) for pan sautéing

Combine all ingredients except for the oil in a medium bowl. Mix well. Heat oil in a spider over a bed of coals. Carefully drop tablespoons of the corn mixture into the hot oil and fry until golden, turning once.

SERVES: 6
HEARTH COOKWARE: A large spider (make do: fry pan on a trivet)
FIRE: coals

Oyster Stew

This is a Thanksgiving staple in our households. A no-fail, no-fuss recipe that is very easy to prepare and staves off hunger pangs that the aroma of roasting turkey teases. This recipe can be doubled for a crowd.

¼ cup (½ stick) butter
2 pints oysters with their liquor
1 quart half-and-half

1 teaspoon salt
1 teaspoon paprika
3 tablespoons parsley, snipped

Melt the butter in a large spider. Add the rest of the ingredients (with the exception of the parsley). Heat until the oysters float and the half and half is hot. Do not overcook as the oysters will toughen. Taste and adjust the seasoning, ladle into mugs or bowls and sprinkle with the fresh parsley.

SERVES: 4 to 6
HEARTH COOKWARE: spider (make do: saucepan on a trivet)
FIRE: coals

Wilted Spring Greens

In the early spring, larders were low and fresh vegetables scarce. A quick sauté of foraged wild greens such as wild spinach (aka Lamb's Quarters), dandelion greens, purslane, stinging nettles, and chickweed was a good way to augment table fare before the garden began producing. These common garden weeds injected much needed vitamins and minerals into the diet. (Tender, domesticated greens: young chard, spinach, and baby arugula, etc. can be substituted in this recipe.)

Large sauté pans with long, sometimes 4-foot handles were constructed for fireplace cooking. Most likely these behemoths were designed to keep the cook a cool distance from the heat and her long, voluminous (combustible) skirts away from the fire. These long-handled collectables are fairly scarce, so rig up a sauté pan on a trivet or use your Dutch oven and wear sensible clothing.

8 cups, loosely packed, mixed wild and/or domestic greens	1 clove garlic (optional)
2 tablespoons olive oil	Sea salt to taste
	Freshly ground black pepper

Thoroughly wash and pick over the greens, discarding any tough stems. Leave water clinging to the greens. Heat 1 tablespoon of the olive oil in a sauté pan (or Dutch oven) placed over hot coals. Add the garlic clove if using and heat for a minute or two to perfume the oil. Remove garlic clove and discard. Add the prepared greens to the pan.

Cover and cook briefly (3 to 5 minutes), stirring once or twice with a spoon, until the greens are barely wilted and still bright green. Drizzle with the additional tablespoon of olive oil. Season with sea salt and freshly ground pepper to taste and serve immediately.

SERVES: 4
HEARTH COOKWARE: long-handled sauté pan on a trivet or Dutch oven (make do: saucepan on a trivet)
FIRE: coals

New England Clam Chowder

Shellfish including lobsters, clams, and oysters were considered "pig" food to the early settlers. Only later did they appreciate these briny delicacies from the sea and incorporate them into their diet.

5 dozen cherrystone clams,
   well scrubbed
5 cups water
5 slices bacon, cut into ¼-inch
   dice
1 cup onions, diced
1 red bell pepper, diced
Whole milk or half and half
   (about 1 cup)
2 cups new potatoes, cubed

2 cups corn kernels, fresh,
   frozen, or canned (if using
   canned, drain)
¼ teaspoon salt
⅛ teaspoon freshly ground
   black pepper
1 teaspoon dried thyme or two
   teaspoons fresh, minced
Fresh thyme sprigs for
   garnishing bowls (optional)

Place cherrystones in a large gypsy kettle suspended from a crane. Add 5 cups water. Cover and cook over hot fire until the clams have opened. (At least 5 minutes.) Swing kettle away from fire and lift the clams out with a slotted spoon. Discard any that have not opened. Let cooking broth cool. Remove the clam meat from the shells, discarding shells, chop clam meat small, and set aside. Strain the clam broth through cheesecloth and reserve.

Swing the empty gypsy kettle back over the hot fire. Add the bacon and sauté until light brown. Add onion and red bell pepper and sauté lightly. Measure the reserved clam broth and add enough milk or half and half to equal 6 cups of liquid. Add to kettle with potatoes, corn, salt, pepper, and dried thyme. Bring to a simmer and cook until the potatoes are tender. About 10 minutes longer.

Add the clams and cook for 2 to 3 minutes longer.

Ladle the chowder into hot bowls and garnish with fresh thyme sprigs (if desired).

SERVES: 6
HEARTH COOKWARE: gypsy kettle
FIRE: hot

Pumpkin Peanut Soup

Herb gardens for both culinary and medicinal use were essential to the early American household. These gardens were planted with a great variety of herbs. Their many uses were commonly known and the plants were collected and dried for the winter. In this recipe thyme can be substituted for the summer savory.

If the soup is to held for any length of time at the hearth, do not add the light cream, instead, top steaming mugs or bowls of soup with a dollop of whipped, heavy cream.

3 tablespoons butter	¼ cup peanut butter
1 medium onion, medium dice	¼ teaspoon summer savory
2 ribs of celery with tops, medium dice	Salt and freshly ground black pepper to taste
2 sprigs parsley	½ cup light cream
2 cups canned pumpkin	Chopped peanuts for garnish (optional)
3 cups chicken broth	

Melt the butter in a gypsy kettle suspended from a crane. Lightly saute the onion and celery. Add parsley, pumpkin, chicken broth, peanut butter, and summer savory to the kettle and mix well. Bring to a simmer over a hot fire and continue to simmer for 15 minutes, moving the kettle slightly away from the intense heat, so it does not boil. Season with salt and pepper to taste and just before serving add the light cream. Garnish mugs or bowls with chopped peanuts if desired.

SERVES: 6
HEARTH COOKWARE: gypsy kettle
FIRE: hot to medium

Old Hen Chicken Soup with Dumplings

In early America, a chicken did not reach the stew pot for soup or fricassee until she had stopped laying eggs. An old hen by this time, she was a tough bird, but made the best-ever chicken soup. To reproduce this full-flavored chicken soup, ask your supermarket butcher for a stewing hen or fowl. This is a good recipe to do on the coldest of winter days since it requires a sustained hot fire for two hours.

1 soup chicken (about 4 to 6 pounds), cut up
Coarse (kosher) salt
1 large onion, peeled, trimmed and the root end scored
5 celery stalks, tops cut off and reserved, cut into inch-thick slices

2 large yams peeled and quartered
1 medium celery root, peeled and cut into quarters
4 parsnips, peeled, trimmed and cut into inch-thick slices
4 carrots, peeled, trimmed and cut into inch-thick slices
1 large bunch dill, rinsed

Rub chicken pieces with about 2 tablespoons coarse salt and set aside in a large bowl while you prepare the vegetables. Tie the celery tops and dill with butchers' twine or string.

Place the vegetables in a large gypsy kettle hung on a crane. Rinse the chicken parts and place over the vegetables. Top with the bundled celery tops and dill. Fill kettle with cold water covering the ingredients by about 1 inch. Partially cover the kettle and heat over a hot fire to the boiling point. Skim. Stir in 2 tablespoons salt, move crane away from the hottest part of the fire, and cook the soup at a simmer for 2 hours, skimming as needed.

To serve: Discard celery tops and dill and whole onion. Remove and set aside chicken pieces. (They will have little or no flavor, so you may want to discard them too.) Strain the soup through a cheesecloth, saving the cooked vegetables to add to the individual soup bowls, if desired. Correct seasoning.

SERVES: 6
HEARTH COOKWARE: gypsy kettle
FIRE: hot

Dumplings

The classic accompaniment to chicken soup. Other herbs from your garden may be added such as summer savory, thyme or sage. Other flavorings such as caraway seed or ¼ cup grated cheese are good variations too.

1½ cups flour	¾ cup milk
2 teaspoons baking powder	1 tablespoon parsley, snipped
¾ teaspoon salt	

In a medium bowl, whisk together flour, baking powder, and salt. Stir in milk and parsley until blended. Drop by the tablespoon onto gently bubbling chicken soup (or stew). Cook for 10 minutes uncovered. Then cover and cook for 10 minutes more.

Mulled Cider

This recipe can be changed to suit your whim or larder. A lemon can be used instead of the orange or apple or combined with them. A cinnamon stick, grated nutmeg, or a dash of applejack can be added to each cup as it is served. (Indian groceries are a good source for inexpensive cinnamon sticks.)

1 orange or apple, peeled	Cinnamon sticks
6 cloves	Nutmeg, freshly grated (optional)
Apple cider to fill gypsy kettle to ¾ full (about 1 gallon)	

Stud an orange (or apple) with the cloves. Hang kettle from crane and fill to ¾ capacity with cider. Add clove-studded fruit and bring to a simmer over hot fire. Swing the crane away from intense heat once the cider reaches a simmer. Ladle hot cider into mugs and serve with cinnamon stick stirrers and freshly grated nutmeg, if desired.

SERVES: 10 to 12, depending on size of kettle
HEARTH COOKWARE: gypsy kettle
FIRE: hot

Hot Cranberry Punch

Cranberries are a new world food and a big commercial crop in New Jersey where we hail from. If you wish to cut the apples ahead, rub the wedges with a cut lemon to keep them from discoloring.

1 quart cranberry juice	4 cloves
1 quart apple juice	1 lemon, thinly sliced
1 cup pear juice	2 apples cored and cut into wedges
1 cinnamon stick	

Hang a gypsy kettle on the crane. Add cranberry, apple, and pear juices, spices, and lemon slices. Stir well. Swing crane, so that the kettle is suspended over the hottest part of the fire. Bring punch to a boiling point. Reduce heat by swinging crane forward to edge of fire and simmer punch for 5 minutes. Ladle into mugs garnished with an apple wedge.

SERVES: 8
HEARTH COOKWARE: gypsy kettle
FIRE: hot

Main Plates and Sides

Garden Squash Frittata

A frittata is a savory, puffy omelet that is baked. Like an omelet, it can hold many fillings. Mushrooms, tomatoes, cheese – even smoked salmon, are just a few of the other possibilities.

5 eggs
1 tablespoon butter
1 tablespoon oil
1 large onion, coarsely chopped
1 small zucchini, trimmed and thinly sliced

1 small summer (yellow) squash, trimmed and thinly sliced
1 tablespoon parsley, snipped
½ teaspoon thyme
Salt and freshly ground black pepper

Beat eggs lightly with a fork in a medium bowl. Melt the butter and oil in a large spider and place over hot coals. Add onion, zucchini, and squash, and sauté until vegetables are golden brown. Add parsley, thyme, and salt and pepper to taste. Pour eggs over the vegetables and allow to set, stir occasionally with a fork so uncooked eggs run to the bottom of the pan. Cover with a lid to set top of eggs.

Cook until eggs are done. Cut into wedges and serve.

SERVES: 4
HEARTH COOKWARE: spider or Dutch oven, (make do: frying pan on a trivet)
FIRE: coals

Onion Tart

Also known as a quiche, fillings can run the gamut from spinach and asparagus to bacon and smoked salmon. Gruyère, Jarlsberg, or Emmenthaler cheeses are especially good in this. And for ease of preparation, you can prebake the pie shell in your kitchen oven, but the fireplace Dutch oven will work too. Depending on how large you cut the wedges, this tart can serve as an appetizer or main course.

¼ cup butter
1½ cups sliced onions – a mixture
   of leeks, yellow, and shallots
Salt
Freshly ground black pepper

1½ cups Swiss cheese, roughly grated
1 partially baked, 9-inch pie shell
4 eggs
2 cups heavy cream
Nutmeg, freshly grated

Preheat Dutch oven with a rack.

Melt butter in a spider and slowly saute onions until golden. Season with salt and pepper to taste.

Spread onions evenly in the pie shell. Sprinkle on the cheese.

In a medium bowl, lightly beat the eggs. Add the cream, salt and pepper to taste and mix well. Place the pie shell with the onion and cheese on the rack in the Dutch oven. Gently pour in egg and cream mixture. Grate a bit of fresh nutmeg on the surface and bake until puffy or until a sharp knife inserted in the center comes out clean, about 30 minutes. (Place slightly more coals underneath the oven at the outset of the baking to set the bottom,)

Allow tart to cool 5 minutes before cutting.

SERVES: 4 as a main course (more as a starter)
HEARTH COOKWARE: Dutch oven with rack
FIRE: coals

Raclette

Serving Raclette on New Year's Eve is a Swiss tradition that is supposed to bring good luck. Raclette cheese, available from gourmet cheese purveyors, has a special melting quality. If not available, Gruyère or Tilsit may be substituted.

3 pounds small red bliss potatoes, washed	Sweet and dill gherkins
3-pound wedge of Raclette cheese	Pickled vegetables

Boil the potatoes in a gypsy kettle suspended from a crane until tender, about 15 minutes. Remove from water with a slotted spoon and drain. Divide the potatoes on 6 to 8 plates and keep warm by the fire's edge.

Remove the rind from the cheese and place on a foil-covered gridiron. Place close to hot coals or fire. As the face of cheese softens and melts, scrape it off with a knife and place on one of the plates next to the potatoes. Repeat for each serving. Watch the cheese closely, as it melts very quickly.

Pass small bowls of gherkins and pickled vegetables.

SERVES: 6 to 8
HEARTH COOKWARE: gypsy kettle, gridiron (make do: Tuscan grill)
FIRE: moderate

Green Lip Mussel Stew

Now that they are farmed, fresh mussels are a joy to cook. No more de-bearding and gritty sand to deal with , as when we gathered them off our dock in Maine. This is the classic Marche aux Puce rendition with cream, but the cream can be omitted and tomatoes used in its stead. Onions can be substituted for the shallots. And half water and white vermouth can be used in place of the wine. A baguette of crusty French bread warmed by the fire is a natural for sopping up the savory juices. Green Lip mussels are especially pretty, as their shells are edged in bright green.

3 tablespoons butter	¾ cup dry white wine
1 large clove garlic, minced	1 small bay leaf
3 tablespoons shallots, small dice	Salt
2-pound bag of fresh mussels,	Freshly ground black pepper
washed and any beards snipped	½ cup heavy cream
off, preferably Green Lip	3 tablespoons parsley, snipped

Melt the butter in a gypsy kettle suspended on a crane. Add garlic and shallots and slowly cook in the butter over low fire until wilted, about 3 minutes. Add mussels to the kettle with the wine, bay leaf, and salt and pepper to taste. Swing crane into the fire to raise heat. Cover and simmer gently until mussels open, 10 to 15 minutes. Pour cream over the mussels and heat until just warm. Ladle stew into bowls and sprinkle with parsley.

SERVES: 4
HEARTH COOKWARE: gypsy kettle
FIRE: moderate to hot

Chicken Pot Pie

A tasty way to use up leftover roast chicken. (A rotisserie chicken from the supermarket is another quick shortcut if you are making this from scratch. So is using prepared pie or biscuit dough.) A little diced ham is also a wonderful addition that Southern cooks swear by. To make an egg wash, stir together 1 lightly beaten egg with 1 teaspoon of water.

1 small (3½ pound) chicken,
  rinsed in cold water
2 stalks celery, trimmed and cut
  in large dice
2 medium carrots, peeled and
  sliced
1 medium onion, peeled and cut
  into eighths
2 teaspoons salt
½ teaspoon fresh ground black
  pepper

3 tablespoons butter
½ cup mushrooms, sliced
3 tablespoons flour
2 tablespoons fresh parsley,
  snipped
¼ teaspoon thyme
1 cup slivered almonds (optional)
Biscuit or pie dough for top crust
Egg wash (optional)

Place the chicken and giblets with the celery, carrots and onion in a gypsy kettle suspended from a crane. Barely cover with cold water and add salt and pepper. Cover pot, swing into the heat of the fire, and bring to a boil, skimming top as needed. Simmer (by swinging the pot slightly away from the heart of the fire) until chicken is fully cooked, yet tender, 30 to 45 minutes longer. Remove chicken and set aside to cool. Remove vegetables and place in a casserole (or deep pie plate) that will fit in your Dutch oven. Reserve chicken broth.

When the chicken has cooled, shred or cut meat into fairly large pieces, discarding the skin and bones. Add to casserole with the vegetables. Preheat Dutch oven fitted with a rack.

Melt butter in a spider over hot coals. Sauté mushrooms until brown. Sprinkle with flour and stir until flour is lightly cooked. Add 2 cups of the reserved chicken broth, a little at a time, and cook, stirring constantly, until sauce has thickened. Add parsley, thyme, and almonds (if using) to sauce. Taste and correct seasoning with additional salt and pepper.

Pour into casserole and gently combine with chicken and vegetables, lifting chicken so sauce can seep underneath. Top with biscuit or pie dough, venting top and crimping edges if desired, Brush with egg wash for a pretty finish.

Place casserole in Dutch oven and bake until the crust is a golden brown and chicken filling bubbles, about 30 to 45 minutes. (Place additional hot coals on oven lid last 10 minutes of baking to ensure a nicely browned top crust.)

SERVES: 6
HEARTH COOKWARE: gypsy kettle, spider (make do: saucepan on a
  trivet), Dutch oven
FIRE: hot with coals

Roast Suckling Pig

Unquestionably the pièce de résistance of fireplace cooking, and a spectacular centerpiece for a Christmas feast. In the city, suckling pigs are available from ethnic butchers, especially of German and Italian descent; in the country, try a local farmer. Since a pig, even a suckling one, extended full length is rather long, it will be necessary to build a larger-than-usual, or double, cooking fire for this recipe. For instructions how to do this, see Chapter 2, The Cooking Fire. If you wish to stuff the pig, use a dry stuffing, such as a mixture of rice, nuts and fruits and add additional cooking time.

1 suckling pig (about 12 pounds)
Fresh cranberries, a small apple, and a bunch of watercress or parsley for
   garnishing
½ cup (1 stick) butter plus ½ cup olive oil melted together for basting

Thread a long spit through the pig's mouth and stomach cavity, and fasten securely with skewers and by tying front and hind legs together with butcher's twine. (This may take some doing, but be sure the pig is well secured, so that it rotates with the spit when it is turned.) Cover ears and tail with foil and wedge a block of wood in its mouth to keep it open. Place before a brisk fire to roast, placing a large drip pan and two reflecting panels in front of it to intensify the fire's heat and to reflect it onto the side of the pig not facing the fire.

Roast the pig, turning and brushing it with the butter and oil mixture frequently until a meat thermometer inserted into its thickest part (a hindquarter) reaches 180 degrees, about 3½ hours. As the pig cooks it may become necessary to cover its belly with foil, since this section will be cooked before the thicker head and hindquarters are done.

To serve: Remove skewers, spit, foil, and wood wedge. Place pig on a large platter or board and garnish, placing cranberries in its eye sockets, an apple in its mouth, and a wreath of parsley or watercress around its neck.

SERVES: 8

HEARTH COOKWARE: Large spit. Use one made expressly for fireplace cooking by a blacksmith as described in the Spit Roasting section of Chapter 4, Roasting, Toasting, Broiling, and Browning Off, (Make do: rent a professional, electric barbecue spit from a party supplier.)

FIRE: double log configuration (see page 26), hot

Filet Mignon Steaks

This is a luxurious dish that would not have appeared on the early American table since cattle were not raised for human consumption. For an authentic touch, substitute Buffalo steaks, now farmed commercially. If not using a Tuscan grill with a built in drip pan, be sure to cover hearth under the gridiron with foil. You can grill any well-marbled steak over coals. Our favorites are rib eye and porterhouse.

6 filet mignon steaks	Salt and freshly ground black pepper
6 shucked oysters	6 or more strips of bacon

Make a small pocket with a sharp knife in one side of each steak. Stuff one oyster in each pocket and season steaks with salt and pepper. Wrap steak in bacon strips securing the bacon with toothpicks, if necessary. Broil over hot coals on a preheated gridiron, turning once, until cooked to desired degree of doneness.

SERVES: 6
HEARTH COOKWARE: gridiron or rotating broiler (make do: Tuscan grill)
FIRE: coals

109

Spit Roasted Small Birds

Song birds were widely consumed in early America. We can only imagine how they tasted! They were grilled in special small tin reflector ovens with hooks. The following recipe designed for a larger reflecting roasting device commonly called a "tin kitchen" is for commercially raised birds such as Cornish hens, poussins and other small game birds such as quail. Adjust cooking times according to size of the bird.

4 Cornish hens	4 cloves garlic
1 lemon cut in half	4 teaspoons tarragon
Salt and freshly ground black pepper	¼ cup butter
	½ cup dry white wine

Rinse birds in cool water and pat dry. Rub insides with cut lemon. Season liberally inside and out with salt and pepper. Place 1 garlic clove and 1 teaspoon tarragon in each cavity. Melt butter in a posnet and add wine to make a basting sauce.

Truss the birds with butcher's twine and thread on a spit, securing with skewers. Roast birds, basting and turning occasionally until skin is nicely browned and thigh juices run clear, about 45 minutes. Split hens and serve half to each guest.

SERVES: 6 to 8

HEARTH COOKWARE: Tin kitchen (make do: spit, reflecting panels, drip pan)

FIRE: Hot

Spit-Roasted Spring Chicken

A simple preparation that demonstrates the versatility and ease of using a tin kitchen. Change the seasonings to suit your taste and your fowl to duck as desired. If you have a hunter in the family, try game birds. And add some fruit wood to your fire for a special taste treat. Alternately, the chicken can be seasoned with fresh rosemary and thyme, now available year round in local supermarkets.

One 3½ pound chicken	2 teaspoons, freshly ground
1 small lemon, cut in half	black pepper
and seeded	2 tablespoons herbs de Provence or
1½ tablespoons coarse salt	fresh thyme and rosemary sprigs

Rinse chicken inside and out with cold running water. Pat dry with paper towels. Rub inside of the chicken with cut lemon halves, leaving as much squeezed juice in the cavity as possible. In a small bowl, mix the salt and pepper together. Rub inside of the chicken with the mixture.

Truss the chicken with butcher's twine and sprinkle top liberally with the herbs de Provence. (If using fresh herbs: place 3 sprigs of thyme and 1 of rosemary in the chicken cavity before you truss the bird.)

Spit the chicken and place in the tin kitchen about 1 to 1½ feet from a hot fire. Let brown and change the spit position as needed to brown all sides nicely (about every 10 to 15 minutes). Adjust the distance from the fire as needed, too. Total cooking time is about 45 minutes.

Cooking juices can be poured off from the bottom of the "kitchen" from its side spout, defatted and served as a simple gravy. If using fresh herbs for seasoning, decorate the chicken on a platter with extras.

SERVES: 4
HEARTH COOKWARE: tin kitchen (make do: hang chicken with butchers twine from crane or hook.)
FIRE: medium high to hot

Planked Shad Fillets

Any firm fish fillets such as trout or salmon or small whole fish can be cooked this way. Use an aromatic wood plank such as untreated cherry or maple. See Chapter 10, Hearth Cookware and Accessories, for sources. About a dozen 1-inch common nails of medium thickness, with or without heads, are needed for this recipe. Covering the hearth with a sheet of foil is a good idea, in case the fish drips. Chapter 4, Roasting, Toasting, Broiling, and Browning Off, gives additional directions on planking a fish.

¼ cup butter	1 lemon cut into wedges for
2 shad fillets	garnishing
Salt and freshly ground black	Parsley sprigs for garnishing
pepper	

Melt butter in a posnet and lightly brush shad fillets on both sides. Secure fish to the plank, skin side down by gently nailing the fillet around the perimeter. (Just barely tack the fish to the board for easy removal later without tearing the flesh.) Season the fillets with salt and pepper to taste and prop before a brisk fire to cook. Turn plank halfway through cooking, so that the top is now in the bottom position. This will ensure that both ends of the fish cook evenly. Roast until fish flakes easily, basting with more butter if necessary, so that shad does not dry out. Do not overcook.

To serve: remove nails and garnish plank with parsley and lemon wedges.

Serves: 2
Hearth cookware: posnet (make do: saucepan on a trivet); clean, hardwood board; common nails
Fire: Medium high to hot

Crab Cakes

Downsizing these crab cakes to silver dollar size turns them into an elegant appetizer or first course.

1 teaspoon Dijon mustard	12 ounces lump crabmeat
1 heaping tablespoon mayonnaise	1 tablespoon snipped chives
1 egg	Salt and freshly ground
¼ cup fine (preferably fresh)	black pepper
bread crumbs	Butter for sautéing

In a medium bowl, whisk together the mustard, mayonnaise, and egg. Mix in the bread crumbs, add the crab meat, chives, salt and pepper to taste, and mix well.

With wet hands, form eight crab cakes with the mixture and sauté cakes in hot butter in a spider, turning once, until nicely browned on both sides.

SERVES: 4
HEARTH COOKWARE: spider (make do: fry pan on a trivet)
FIRE: coals

Fresh Cranberry Relish

This is another Thanksgiving staple. Cranberries freeze beautifully, so we buy extra bags in November when they are plentiful in the supermarket and freeze them for later. This recipe makes enough for Thanksgiving dinner plus perhaps even some leftovers to put on your turkey sandwiches the next day.

Two 12-ounce bags fresh cranber-	1½ cups sugar
ries, washed and picked over	Grated rind of 1 orange
(discard any shriveled or	Juice of 1 orange, plus water to
white berries)	equal 1 cup

Combine all the ingredients in a large spider and cook, stirring occasionally, until the cranberries pop open, about 10 minutes. Skim off foam from top. Serve warm or refrigerate if you want the sauce to gel a bit.

SERVES: 8 to 12
HEARTH COOKWARE: spider (make do: saucepan on a trivet)
FIRE: coals

Yankee Baked Beans

These were a typical overnight dish cooked in the dregs of the beehive oven heat, but they are also fine cooked in a Dutch oven. Pea, marrow, Great Northern, lima or navy beans can be used in this recipe. You will need a Dutch oven large enough to accommodate a 2½ quart casserole to make this recipe.

1 pound or 2 cups dried beans, rinsed, picked over, and soaked overnight in cold water to cover by 2 inches	1 teaspoon dry mustard
	1 teaspoon salt
	1 tablespoon cider vinegar
	¼ teaspoon ground cloves
½ cup molasses	1 large onion, chopped
¼ cup brown sugar	½ pound salt pork, scored

Drain presoaked beans, add to a gypsy kettle suspended from a crane and add cold water to cover. Swing kettle over fire and simmer beans for 30 minutes. Drain beans, reserving liquid. Place beans in a 2½ quart casserole (with lid).

In a bowl, combine 1 cup of the reserved liquid, molasses, brown sugar, mustard, salt, vinegar, cloves, and onion. Stir into beans. Bury salt pork in the beans and add additional reserved liquid to cover beans.

Cover casserole and bake in a preheated Dutch oven over medium heat until beans are tender, 3 to 5 hours, adding more of the reserved liquid as needed. To give a nice glaze to the beans, during last ½ hour of cooking, remove the casserole cover and bring salt pork to the top.

SERVES: 4 to 6
HEARTH COOKWARE: gypsy kettle, Dutch oven with rack
FIRE: coals

Ember Baked Spuds

The simplest of all recipes. More or less potatoes can be baked, depending on the heads sitting around the fire. Yams are delicious baked this way too.

6 baking potatoes such as Idaho	Chives, chopped (optional)
Pats of butter	Crisp bacon, crumbled (optional)
Sour cream	

Pierce potatoes, wrap in two layers of foil, and bake in the fire's embers until cooked through. (Test with a wood skewer or cake tester for doneness.) Unwrap potatoes and leave before the fire on the hot hearth stones to crisp up the skins for 5 minutes longer.

Split and top with butter and/or sour cream, garnishing with chives and/or bacon, if desired.

SERVES: 6
HEARTH COOKWARE: tin foil
FIRE: coals

Roasted Herbed Tomatoes

Even "winter"tomatoes taste good this way; roasting seems to coax out their flavor. In this recipe, one cup of cooked rice can be substituted for the bread crumbs.

3 medium to large, firm, ripe tomatoes	1 tablespoon parsley, snipped
1 cup fresh breadcrumbs	Salt and freshly ground black pepper
2 tablespoons olive oil, plus additional for drizzling on tomatoes	¼ cup Parmesan cheese, grated (optional)
1 large clove garlic, minced	

Cut tomatoes in half crosswise. Gently remove juice and seeds with your fingers. With a small knife, trim away stem end. Mix breadcrumbs, 2 tablespoons olive oil, garlic, parsley, salt and pepper to taste. Top tomatoes with bread crumb mixture and grated parmesan cheese (if used). Drizzle additional oil on top of tomatoes and place in a pie plate in a preheated Dutch oven fitted with a rack.

Bake until tomatoes are heated through, slightly softened, and breadcrumbs begin to brown, about 15 to 20 minutes.

SERVES: 4 to 6
HEARTH COOKWARE: Dutch oven with a rack
FIRE: coals

Sweet Potato Pie

A sometime dessert in the South. We've reduced the sugar making it a suitable vegetable to serve with roast pork, turkey, chicken, etc. A pre-made pie shell is fine for this recipe, but if you are making the pastry yourself, use the pastry trimmings to decorate the top of the pie. For Thanksgiving, pumpkins or maple leaves cut from the dough are a festive touch.

2 pounds sweet potatoes	1 teaspoon vanilla
¾ cup butter, softened	¼ teaspoon nutmeg
3 eggs	½ teaspoon cinnamon
1 tablespoon brown sugar	One 9-inch pie shell, unbaked
½ teaspoon baking powder	

Boil sweet potatoes in water a gypsy kettle suspended from a crane, skins on, until tender. (Alternately they can be pricked, wrapped in foil, and roasted in the fire's embers.

Preheat Dutch oven fitted with rack.

When sweet potatoes are cool enough to handle, peel and mash in a large bowl with the softened butter. Add eggs, brown sugar, baking powder, vanilla, and spices and mix well.

Place pie shell in preheated oven. Pour in sweet potato filling, smoothing off top with a spatula. Bake until a knife or toothpick inserted in the center comes out clean, about 45 minutes.

SERVES: 6 to 8
HEARTH COOKWARE: gypsy kettle (optional), Dutch oven
FIRE: hot with coals

Scones, Muffins, Breads, and Biscuits

Bannocks

A hearty oatmeal pancake of Scottish origin, popular in early America. To sour milk, add 1 teaspoon lemon juice or vinegar to 1 cup of milk. Let stand 10 minutes.

2 cups rolled oats	1 teaspoon bacon fat or melted butter plus
1 teaspoon salt	additional butter for greasing the griddle
1 teaspoon baking soda	1 tablespoon maple syrup
1 cup buttermilk or sour milk	2 eggs, lightly beaten

Preheat a hanging griddle suspended from a crane by swinging it into the fire.

In a large bowl, combine oats, salt, and baking soda. Stir in the buttermilk, bacon fat, and maple syrup. Add the eggs and mix all the ingredients together thoroughly.

Grease the griddle with butter and place spoonfuls of batter on it. Bake the bannocks, turning once with a spatula, approximately 3 minutes on each side.

SERVES: 4

HEARTH COOKWARE: posnet for melting butter (make do: small saucepan on a trivet), hanging griddle

FIRE: moderate to hot

Perfect Corn Bread

This recipe is especially fun to do with children. The youngest ones can gather the maple leaves, which serve as an early American "parchment paper liner" (either green or turned autumn leaves work fine, as long as they aren't dried out), while the older ones mix the batter. Maple leaf stems also provide the perfect handles for removing the leaves at the end of baking and the leaf shape leaves a pretty pattern. (Two layers of brown paper cut from a grocery bag, and fitted to the bottom of the Dutch oven can also be used. Grease the top layer.)

To pair this recipe with a bowl of chili, add all or any of the following: canned (drained) or frozen corn niblets, crumbled bacon, green chilies (fresh or canned).

¼ cup butter, melted	1 cup yellow cornmeal
1 cup flour	1 cup milk
¼ cup sugar	2 eggs
4 teaspoons baking powder	Large, fresh maple leaves to line
¾ teaspoons salt	bottom of Dutch oven

Preheat Dutch oven and melt butter in a posnet.

In a large bowl whisk together the flour, sugar, baking powder, and salt. Add the cornmeal and whisk again. Add melted butter to the dry ingredients.

In a small bowl lightly beat together milk and eggs. Add to the dry ingredients and mix until just moistened. Do not overbeat.

Carefully, so as not to burn fingers, line the bottom of the Dutch oven with maple leaves (or two layers of greased brown paper). Pour the cornbread mixture over the maple leaves and bake until a knife or toothpick inserted in the center comes out clean, about 20 to 25 minutes.

Remove Dutch oven lid and let corn bread cool slightly, before turning out on a wooden cutting board. Pull off the maple leaves by their stems. Cut in wedges and serve.

SERVES: 6 to 8

HEARTH COOKWARE: posnet (make do: small saucepan on a trivet), Dutch oven

FIRE: coals

Oatmeal Cinnamon Bread

This fragrant bread is the perfect thing to do on a winter's day, when you're snowed in and curled up by the fire. The warm hearth is a fine place to allow yeast breads to rise. But take care not to put your dough too close to the fire or its embers. Too intense a heat will kill the growing (rising) yeast. Both loaves can be baked at once by stacking two Dutch ovens on top of each other, or in one very large Dutch oven.

1 cup milk, scalded	1 package dry yeast
½ cup butter (1 stick), melted, plus additional melted butter for brushing tops of bread	¼ cup lukewarm water
	4 cups flour
	2 cups rolled oats
¼ cup sugar	2 eggs, lightly beaten
1½ teaspoons salt	Cinnamon

Make bread dough: Scald milk in a spider. Melt butter in a posnet. In a small bowl, stir together milk, butter, sugar, and salt. Cool mixture to lukewarm. Sprinkle yeast over lukewarm water to proof. In a large bowl mix together 1 cup of the flour and all of the oats. Stir in milk mixture, lightly beaten eggs, and dissolved yeast. Add remaining flour and mix well. Turn out dough onto a floured board and knead until smooth and elastic. Place in a large greased bowl and turn dough over a few times to grease top.

Cover and let rise in a warm spot until double in bulk–about 1½ hours. Punch dough down, turn onto the floured board, and let rest 10 minutes. Divide dough in half. Roll each half into a rectangle and lightly dust with cinnamon. Re-roll and put each coil into greased bread loaf pans. Let rise until double in bulk, about 30 minutes.

When loaves have risen, preheat Dutch oven with a rack, brush tops of breads with melted butter and bake each separately in the oven, until done, about 40 minutes. (A hollow sound can be heard when you rap your knuckles on the top.) During latter part of baking, pile slightly more coals on oven lid to brown top crust nicely.

MAKES: 2 loaves
HEARTH COOKWARE: spider and posnet (make do: small saucepans on a trivet); 1 or 2 Dutch oven(s) with rack(s)
FIRE: hot, coals

Fragrant Herb Bread

Another yeast bread to bake by the fire. This one is more like a savory focaccia, rather than a sweet bread. See prior Oatmeal bread recipe (page 117) for tips on rising dough by the fire, baking both breads at once, and achieving a nicely browned crust.

2 packages dry yeast
½ cup plus 1 cup lukewarm water
Pinch of sugar
4 cups flour, plus additional flour
   if needed
2 teaspoons salt
Butter for greasing bowl and
   brown paper

¼ cup olive oil
1 tablespoon dried sage, rosemary,
   or dill weed, plus additional
   for sprinkling tops
Brown paper circles to fit Dutch
   oven, greased
Kosher or coarse salt

To make dough: Proof yeast by dissolving in ½ cup lukewarm water with a pinch of sugar. In a large bowl, whisk together flour and salt. Make a well in the center of the flour and add dissolved yeast mixture and additional cup of lukewarm water. Stir gently, allowing flour to gradually work into the dough. Transfer mixture to a floured board and knead until smooth and satiny. Add additional flour if needed. Form into a ball and place in a greased bowl, turning ball a few times, until all surfaces are greased. Cover and let rise in a warm place until double in bulk, about 1 hour.

Punch dough down and work in olive oil and herbs. Knead until smooth on a floured board. Cut dough in half and roll or pat out each half into a circle on paper liners. (Dough circles should be slightly smaller than circumference of the paper liners.) Cover and allow to rise until double in bulk, about 45 minutes.

Preheat Dutch oven. Prick breads with a fork in 5 to 6 places. Sprinkle lightly with additional herbs and coarse salt and bake one at a time, placing bread on paper circle in oven and baking until done (about 25 minutes). Keep second loaf out of draft, but not too close to the heat until first bread is done.

MAKES: 2 flatbreads
FIREPLACE COOKWARE: Dutch oven
FIRE: coals

Boston Brown Bread

This is a steamed bread that goes well with the baked beans recipe (page 114). To sour milk: add 1 teaspoon lemon juice or vinegar to 1 cup milk. Let stand 10 minutes. Keep a filled teakettle on the hearth so that boiling water is readily available.

½ cup flour	½ cup yellow cornmeal
½ teaspoon baking soda	½ cup whole wheat flour
½ teaspoon salt	1 cup sour milk
1 teaspoon cinnamon	¼ cup molasses
2 tablespoons sugar	½ cup raisins

In a large bowl, whisk together flour, baking soda, salt, and cinnamon. Whisk in sugar, cornmeal, and whole wheat flour. Add milk, molasses, and raisins, stirring until just blended. Pour into a well-greased, 1-pound coffee can lined with a circle of greased waxed paper at the bottom. Cover can with greased waxed paper or aluminum foil and tie securely with string.

Place can on a rack in a gypsy kettle. Add boiling water to reach halfway up the side of the can. Cover kettle and steam about 3 hours, replenishing water if it boils away. (Aways replenish with boiling water.) When done, the bread will have risen and a cake tester inserted in the center will come out clean. Remove bread from the can while still hot. Serve warm with butter or cream cheese.

MAKES: 1 loaf
HEARTH COOKWARE: gypsy kettle with rack and lid
FIRE: hot

Cornmeal Biscuits

Sharp cheddar cheese roughly grated, finely minced cooked ham, or snipped chives can be used in place of the bacon.

⅓ cup crumbled bacon
1½ cups flour
½ cup cornmeal
2½ teaspoons baking powder
1 teaspoon salt

⅓ cup butter cut in small pieces
plus additional butter to grease
griddle
⅔ cup light cream

Cook bacon in a spider. Drain on paper towels, crumble, and set aside.

Preheat hanging griddle over the fire.

In a large bowl, whisk together the flour, cornmeal, baking powder, salt. Mix in the crumbled bacon. Blend in the butter with a pastry blender or your finger tips until the mixture is the consistency of rough cornmeal. Slowly stir in cream with a fork until a soft dough is formed.

Turn out dough onto a floured board and knead just until a smooth dough is achieved. (Do not overdo the kneading.) Roll dough out on the board until it is ½-inch thick. Cut biscuits using a 1½-inch, floured cutter. Grease the griddle with butter, wiping off any excess pools of shortening, and place half of the biscuits on the griddle to bake. Bake until they have risen and are a delicate brown on one side. Turn and brown on the other side, about 5 to 7 minutes on each side. Remove baked biscuits and bake second batch.

MAKES: 1½ dozen biscuits
HEARTH COOKWARE: spider (make do: skillet on trivet), hanging griddle
FIRE: hot, coals

Strawberry-Rhubarb Scones

These are wonderful with homemade strawberry jam and/or clotted cream. For dessert, the scones can be dressed up with fresh strawberries and whipped cream.

2 cups flour

3 tablespoons sugar, plus additional for sprinkling tops

1 tablespoon baking powder

3/4 teaspoon salt

6 tablespoons, cold unsalted butter, cut into pieces

1 cup strawberries, hulled and cut into quarters

1 cup red rhubarb stalk, cut into 1-inch pieces

Zest of 1 lemon, grated

1/3 cup heavy cream, plus additional for brushing tops

2 eggs, lightly beaten

Preheat a Dutch oven fitted with a rack.

In a large bowl, whisk together the dry ingredients. With your fingers or a pastry cutter, blend in the butter until it forms small peas. Stir in strawberries, rhubarb, and lemon zest.

In a small bowl mix cream and eggs together . Make a well in the dry ingredients and add liquid all at once. Mix with a fork just until dough comes together. Turn out onto a board or counter and knead a few times to mix well. (Do not overdo the kneading. The less the better for tender scones.)

Pat dough into a circle about 1 to 1½ inches thick. Cut into 6 wedges and transfer to a layer of heavy duty foil. Place on the rack in your Dutch oven. Brush tops with cream and sprinkle with sugar. Bake for 20 to 25 minutes or until golden brown. Remove scones from oven and cool on a rack before serving.

MAKES: 6 large scones
HEARTH COOKWARE: Dutch oven with rack
FIRE: coals

Cakes, Cookies, Pies, and Puddings

Hand-Peeled Apple Pie

This pie freezes perfectly before it is baked. We often assemble a slew of these pies in the fall when apples are at their peak and tuck them away in a chest freezer for a bitter winter day. To bake: Unwrap and brush the top of the frozen pie with an egg wash (see recipe), sprinkle with a tablespoon or two of sugar, and pop in a preheated Dutch oven. Adjust the sugar in the filling to your taste. Reducing the sugar allows the taste of the fruit to shine through.

¼ cup sugar	Juice of 1 lemon
1 tablespoon flour	1 tablespoon butter, cut into bits
⅛ teaspoon salt	1 egg
Grated rind of 1 lemon	1 teaspoon water
¼ teaspoon nutmeg	Pastry for a a two crust,
½ teaspoon cinnamon	9-inch pie
2½ pounds baking apples, peeled,	(recipe follows)
cored, and cut into thick wedges	

Preheat Dutch oven with a rack.

In a small bowl combine sugar, flour, salt, lemon rind, nutmeg, and cinnamon. In a large bowl toss the apples with the lemon juice to keep them from discoloring. Sprinkle on the sugar mixture and toss again to coat evenly.

Roll out bottom pie crust and line pie plate. Heap apples in the center of the crust, dot with the butter and cover with top crust, crimping edges as desired, and cutting slits in top so that steam can escape.

Make a wash by beating the egg and water together in a small dish and brush on pie crust just before baking.

Bake in a preheated Dutch oven until top crust is golden brown and apples.

.bubbling, about 40 minutes. Pile slightly more coals under the Dutch oven during the first 15 minutes to set the bottom crust, and slightly more on top during the last 15 minutes to nicely brown the top.

MAKES: 1 pie
HEARTH COOKWARE: Dutch oven with rack
FIRE: coals

Basic Pie Crust Pastry

This recipe makes enough for one, 9-inch two-crust pie or two, 9-inch one-crust pies. In a pinch there are very good, all natural, ready-made pie crusts available in your supermarket freezer and refrigerated cases. Omit the sugar if you wish to use the dough for a quiche shell, and don't overwork your pie dough or it will toughen. Crisco stick shortening is perfect for this recipe and easy to measure. This dough can be made ahead and frozen until needed. Defrost in your refrigerator.

1½ cups flour
½ teaspoon salt
1 tablespoon sugar
8 tablespoons (one stick) cold
    butter, cut into bits

4 tablespoons cold vegetable
    shortening
2 to 3 tablespoons ice water

Whisk together in a large bowl the flour, salt, and sugar. Add the butter and blend with a pastry blender or your finger tips until the butter forms small peas. Add the shortening and blend until just incorporated. Add ice water a tablespoon at a time until dough begins to form a ball. Gather dough together. Divide dough and shape into two disks. Wrap each in plastic wrap and refrigerate for at least 1 hour to allow dough to rest. When ready to bake pie, roll out (one crust at a time) on a floured board.

MAKES: one, 9-inch two-crust pie or two, 9-inch one-crust pies

Pecan Pie

Use the recipe for the one-crust pie pastry on page 125. Wild hickory nuts can be substituted for pecans. While they are delicious, they are very difficult to shell and almost none will come out perfect enough to decorate the top. If using, increase the overall nut pieces to 2¼ cups and enjoy the taste. For a flavor boost, add a tablespoon of bourbon or apple jack to the pie.

4 eggs	2 cups pecan pieces plus 10 to 12
¾ cup sugar	unbroken halves for decorating
½ teaspoon salt	top
¾ cup light corn syrup	1 unbaked pie shell
1 tablespoon butter	Whipped cream
1 tablespoon vanilla	

Preheat Dutch oven with a rack.

In a medium bowl, beat eggs lightly and add sugar, salt, and corn syrup. Melt the tablespoon of butter in a large, long-handled metal spoon held over embers or near the fire. Stir in the melted butter and the vanilla and mix well.

Spread the pecan pieces in the bottom of the unbaked pie shell and place in the Dutch oven. Pour the pie filling over the nuts and float the perfect halves in a pattern on the top of the pie.

Bake, spreading more coals under the pie during the first 15 minutes of baking to set the bottom, for a total of 30 to 40 minutes. A cake tester or toothpick should come out clean when the pie is done. Plate with whipped cream.

MAKES: 1 pie

HEARTH COOKWARE: Dutch oven with rack; large, long-handled metal spoon

FIRE: coals

Wild Blueberry Tart

If you can get them, the small, low bush blueberries that grow wild in Maine have the most flavor. Some supermarkets carry Wyman's fresh frozen wild blueberries. But finish the pie with fat, juicy Jersey (or other cultivated) blueberries. They have more eye appeal.

Cookie Dough Crust
1 cup flour
2 tablespoons sugar
¼ teaspoon salt
½ cup (1 stick) unsalted, refrigerated butter
1 tablespoon cider vinegar or ice water

Filling
3 cups frozen or fresh blueberries
⅓ cup sugar
2 tablespoons flour
1 tablespoon grated lemon zest

Topping
2 cups fresh blueberries

Preheat Dutch oven with a rack.

Make the cookie dough crust: Whisk together the flour, sugar and salt. Cut butter into small pieces and blend into flour mixture with your fingers until butter is pea-sized. Mix in vinegar or water and gather dough into a ball. Press dough into a small metal pie plate with your fingers, pushing dough slightly up the sides of the pan. Flatten top edges with your finger or a knife.

Mix together the filling ingredients and pour into the pie shell. Bake in preheated Dutch oven, replenishing the coals as needed, for 30 minutes or until the blueberries are bubbling and the pie crust is nicely browned.

Remove from Dutch oven to a baking rack or fireplace trivet and immediately spread the fresh blueberries over the top of the hot pie. Cool and serve. (Great with vanilla ice cream or whipped cream.)

MAKES: 1 tart
HEARTH COOKWARE: Dutch oven with rack
FIRE: coals

Apple Blackberry Crisp

This recipe is equally good without the berries, but don't omit the scoop of vanilla ice cream. The yin and the yang of the hot crisp and the cold ice cream is a divine match.

Topping

1 cup flour	2 teaspoons cinnamon
1 cup brown sugar, firmly packed	½ teaspoon nutmeg
¾ cup old-fashioned rolled oats	½ cup (1 stick) unsalted butter,
¾ cup coarsely chopped walnuts	melted

Filling

5 cups baking apples, such as Cortland, Macintosh, or Granny Smith, peeled, quartered, cored and cut into large chunks	1 cup blackberries ½ cup sugar Zest of 1 lemon, grated Juice of 1 lemon, strained Vanilla ice cream Mint sprigs (optional)

Preheat Dutch oven with rack. Butter an ovenproof 6-cup capacity baking dish.

Make the topping: In a medium bowl blend the flour, sugar, rolled oats, walnuts, cinnamon, nutmeg, and melted butter with your fingers or a wooden spoon until it clumps. Set aside.

Prepare the filling: Gently toss apples, blackberries, sugar, lemon zest and juice in a large bowl. Fill pan with the mixture and crumble on topping to thickly cover.

Bake in a Dutch oven until the topping is brown and crispy and the filling is bubbling hot, about 30 to 40 minutes. Serve warm with a scoop of vanilla ice cream and decorate with a sprig of fresh mint, if desired.

SERVES: 8
HEARTH COOKWARE: Dutch oven with rack
FIRE: coals

Apple Coffee Cake

Tea was a more common, even notorious, beverage in early America, but the addition of black coffee gives this cake a wonderful flavor

½ cup (1 stick) butter,
   room temperature
1 cup sugar
2 eggs
1½ cups flour
1 teaspoon baking soda
¾ teaspoon salt

1 teaspoon cinnamon
¾ teaspoon ground cloves
½ cup, cold black coffee
2 cups peeled, shredded apple
1 cup raisins
½ cup coarsely chopped walnuts

Preheat Dutch oven with rack.

In a large bowl, cream the butter with the sugar. Add eggs, one at a time, and beat until fluffy. In a small bowl, whisk together the dry ingredients and add alternately with the coffee to the creamed mixture, beginning and ending with the dry ingredients. Mix in the apple, raisins, and walnuts.

Pour the batter into a greased and floured, 9 x 2-inch round pan. Place on rack in the preheated Dutch oven and bake until a cake tester or toothpick inserted the the center comes out clean, about 1 hour.

MAKES: 1 cake
HEARTH COOKWARE: Dutch oven with rack
FIRE: coals

Soft Gingerbread

This is soft or cake-like gingerbread. Early Americans were also fond of crisp gingerbread cookies and used fanciful, handmade tin cookie cutters to cut out cookies in the shape of farm animals, hearts, birds, leaves, and of course, gingerbread men and women. These cookie cutters are very collectable today. To sour milk, add 1 teaspoon lemon juice or vinegar to 1 cup milk. Let stand 10 minutes.

½ cup sugar
½ cup (1 stick) butter,
   room temperature
1 teaspoon ginger
1 teaspoon cinnamon
½ teaspoon salt
1 egg

¾ cup dark molasses
1 cup sour milk
2 cups flour
1 teaspoon baking soda
Whipped cream or vanilla ice
   cream (optional)

Preheat Dutch oven with rack.

In a large bowl, cream together sugar, butter, ginger, cinnamon, and salt. Add egg and beat until fluffy. Mix in molasses and milk.

In a small bowl, whisk together flour and baking soda. Add to the creamed ingredients, mixing batter until smooth.

Grease and flour a 9-inch square baking pan. Place in preheated Dutch oven and pour gingerbread mixture into the pan. Bake until the top of the cake springs back when touched with your finger, about 30 to 40 minutes. (Pile slightly more coals on top of the oven near the end of baking to brown the top of the gingerbread. Cut into squares when cool and serve with whipped cream or vanilla ice cream, if desired.

MAKES: 8 squares
HEARTH COOKWARE: Dutch oven
FIRE: coals

Brownies

Dust the buttered pan with cocoa, instead of flour for a more compatible color. For more uniform looking brownies trim off the crisp edges of the turned out brownie "cake," before cutting it into squares.

2 squares of unsweetened chocolate	¾ cup flour
⅓ cup butter	½ teaspoon baking powder
1 cup sugar	½ teaspoon salt
2 eggs	½ cup walnuts pieces

Preheat Dutch oven with rack.

Melt chocolate and butter together in a spider over low heat. Pour into a large bowl and stir in sugar and eggs, mixing well. In a small bowl, whisk together flour, baking powder, and salt and add to the chocolate mixture, mixing well. Add walnuts and stir until incorporated.

Place an 8-inch square, buttered and floured pan in the Dutch oven. Pour mixture into pan and bake until a cake tester or toothpick comes out clean, about 30 to 35 minutes. Let cool slightly, turn out onto a cutting board, and cut into 8 to 16 squares.

MAKES: 8 squares
HEARTH COOKWARE: Spider (make do: saucepan on a trivet), Dutch oven with rack
FIRE: coals

Waffles

Early American waffle irons had long handles, so that they could be manipulated at a safe, comfortable distance from the fire. To use a modern iron, place on a trivet over coals and use heavy potholders to protect your hands.

Your waffle iron may have to be re-seasoned if a large batch is made. You'll know when it's time. The waffles start to stick! To re-season: Apply a little more shortening to iron surface and reheat over the fire.

1 cup flour	⅓ cup sugar
1 teaspoon baking powder	1 cup sour cream
1 teaspoon cinnamon	¼ cup butter
4 eggs	

In a small bowl, whisk together flour, baking powder, and cinnamon. In a large bowl, beat together eggs and sugar until thick and lemon-colored. Fold flour and sour cream alternately into the egg and sugar mixture until well blended. Melt the butter in a spider and stir into the batter.

Season the waffle iron with vegetable shortening or melted butter and pre-heat over hot coals, turning so both sides of iron are heated evenly. Pour in waffle batter and bake until the iron no longer steams and the edges of the waffle are golden brown, about 2 minutes. Repeat process until all the batter is used, re-seasoning iron if needed.

MAKES: 4 waffles
HEARTH COOKWARE: spider (make do: saucepan on a trivet), waffle iron
FIRE: coals

Wafers

In early America, these thin "cookies" were made in special, long-handled wafer irons whose flat baking surfaces the blacksmith incised with delicate designs to decorate the finished wafer. There is really no comparable baking device in the contemporary American kitchen. A Pizzelle iron is the closest approximation. One teaspoon of mace can be substituted for the lemon rind. Drops of water should dance on the iron's surface when it is ready for baking. Ricotta cream, ice cream, and/or preserves are other fillings. Use your imagination.

½ cup (1 stick) butter
3 eggs
1 cup sugar
2¼ cups flour

½ teaspoon grated lemon rind
Whipped cream and fresh berries
for filling

Melt the butter in a spider and allow to cool slightly. In a large bowl, beat the eggs and the sugar together until light and fluffy. Stir in the melted butter, flour, and grated lemon rind.

Form balls (or fingers if your iron is rectangular) using one tablespoon of the stiff dough.

Place on a seasoned (with vegetable shortening or butter), preheated iron, squeezing the dough between the iron's plates to form a flat cookie. Cook the wafer until the steam stops, about 2 minutes. Remove the wafer from the iron, (use a knife tip to loosen an edge if needed) curling it up like a cone or tube while it's still hot, if you wish to fill it later. (You can also leave the wafers flat.) Serve filled or topped with whipped cream and fresh berries.

MAKES: two dozen, depending on the size of your wafer iron
FIREPLACE COOKWARE: Spider (make do: saucepan on a trivet), wafer iron
FIRE: coals

S'mores

This is not really a recipe, but an idea. It's an old Girl Scout campfire tradition that translates well to informal fireplace gatherings, especially with children. For a more nutritious variation, spread peanut butter on the graham crackers. The marshmallows can also be toasted on sticks over the fire as they are done at the campsite.

8 whole graham crackers broken in half to form 16 squares	4 small chocolate bars
	8 large marshmallows

Place 8 of the graham cracker squares in a reflector bake oven and top each with a marshmallow. Place the oven in front of the fire and bake until the marshmallows are gooey and slightly browned. Remove to a plate and place half a chocolate bar on each marshmallow. Top with another graham cracker, pressing down slightly, to form a sandwich.

MAKES: 8 (but everyone wants s'more)
HEARTH EQUIPMENT: tin bake oven (make do: sticks)
FIRE: coals

Holiday Plum Pudding

Flaming brandy is the final touch to this traditional Christmas pudding. It takes a long time to make, but fortunately can be made ahead. Keep a teakettle of water boiling on the crane to refill the pudding kettle water when it begins to boil away (below the halfway mark).

3 cups coarse, fresh bread crumbs	½ cup walnut pieces
1 cup milk	½ cup mixed candied fruits
½ cup (1 stick) butter	
One 10-ounce jar peach jam	*Hard Sauce*
1 cup flour	½ cup (1 stick) butter,
1 teaspoon baking soda	room temperature
1 teaspoon salt	½ cup confectioners' sugar
2 teaspoons cinnamon	⅛ cup Grand Marnier
¼ teaspoon allspice	Dash of nutmeg, if desired
¼ teaspoon cloves	

Place a kettle of water to boil at the hearth.

Place the bread crumbs in a large bowl and pour the milk over them. Allow to soak for a few minutes. Meanwhile, melt the butter in a spider and stir in the peach jam.

Sift the flour, baking soda, salt, and spices over the softened bread crumbs and fold in. Add the jam, butter, the nuts and the candied fruits and gently mix in. Pour pudding into a well-greased 1-quart mold. Cover with aluminum foil and secure the foil with string or wire.

Place pudding on a rack in a gypsy kettle suspended from a crane. Add boiling water to reach halfway up the sides of the mold. Cover the kettle with a tight-fitting lid and steam until the pudding tests done with a cake tester, about 3 hours. Add more boiling water as needed to maintain the water level in the kettle.

While pudding is steaming make hard sauce: In a small bowl, cream the butter and sugar well. Add the Grand Marnier a little at a time and beat until light and fluffy. Taste and add a dash of nutmeg if desired. Set hard sauce aside.

When the pudding is cooked, turn out onto a warm serving dish and serve with hard sauce.

SERVES: 8
HEARTH COOKWARE: spider (make do: saucepan on a trivet), gypsy kettle
    with rack and lid, tilting teakettle (make do: teakettle on a trivet)
FIRE: moderate to hot

Apricot and Apple Steamed Pudding

An empty 2-pound coffee can makes an excellent pudding mold for this recipe.

2½ cups flour
1 teaspoon salt
1 teaspoon baking powder
½ teaspoon cinnamon
¼ teaspoon nutmeg
¼ teaspoon ginger
¼ cup butter
¾ cup brown sugar
1 egg
½ cup milk

1 cup shredded apple
½ cup dried apricots, cut in
 quarters
¾ cup walnut pieces
Butter or vegetable shortening
 for greasing mold
Fine bread crumbs for
 dusting mold
Hard sauce, lemon sauce,
 or ice cream

Place a kettle of water to boil at the hearth.

In a small bowl whisk together flour, salt, baking powder, cinnamon, nutmeg, and ginger. In a large bowl, cream together butter and brown sugar. Add egg and cream until well mixed. Stir in half the flour mixture. Add milk and blend. Mix in remaining flour mixture.

Stir apple, apricots, and walnuts into the batter.

Pour the pudding mixture into a well-greased, 6-cup mold that has been dusted with bread crumbs. Cover tightly with greased aluminum foil and tie the cover securely with string or wire. Set on a rack in a gypsy kettle suspended from a crane. Set the pudding on the rack and fill the kettle to halfway up the side of the pudding mold with boiling water. Cover the kettle and steam, until the pudding tests done with a cake tester (about 1½ hours). During cooking, add more boiling water as needed to maintain the water level in the kettle.

To serve: Remove the pudding from the kettle and let stand about 10 minutes, then invert mold on serving platter. (Pudding should have shrunk enough for easy removal.) Slice and serve with hard sauce, lemon sauce, or ice cream.

SERVES: 8 to 10
HEARTH COOKWARE: tilting teakettle or teakettle on a trivet, gypsy
 kettle with rack and lid
FIRE: hot

Pumpkin Pudding

This is an easier pudding to prepare, since it is baked in a soufflé dish, rather than steamed in a kettle of boiling water and the cooking time is only 1 hour. Undiluted, evaporated milk can be used in place of regular milk in this recipe for a creamier, richer taste.

4 eggs
One 13-ounce can pumpkin
2 tablespoons flour
2 tablespoons cornstarch
1 teaspoon salt
1 teaspoon cinnamon

½ teaspoon nutmeg
⅛ teaspoon cloves (optional)
1 cup honey
1 teaspoon vanilla
3 cups milk

Preheat Dutch oven with a rack

In a large bowl, beat eggs well. Mix in the pumpkin. In a small bowl, whisk together all the dry ingredients, then add to the pumpkin mixture with the honey, vanilla, and milk. Mix well. Place a lightly greased, 2-quart soufflé dish on a rack in the Dutch oven and fill with the pumpkin pudding mixture. Bake until a knife inserted in the center comes out clean, about 1 hour.

SERVES: 6
HEARTH COOKWARE: Dutch oven with rack
FIRE: coals

Orchard Applesauce

When apples are in season, we pick or buy them by the bushel at our local farm and make enough sauce for the winter. But even in the dead of winter, cold storage apples, make a superior sauce to the bottled, supermarket brands. For festive occasions, we stir fresh whole raspberries into the finished sauce when serving.

3 pounds Macintosh apples, Juice of 1 lemon, strained
   quartered and cored 1 cinnamon stick
⅓ cup sugar

Cut the apple quarters in half and place in a gypsy kettle. Toss with sugar and lemon juice. Add the cinnamon stick and let stand for 20 to 30 minutes, or until apples have released their juices. Hang the kettle over a hot fire, cover, and let cook until the apple juices begin to bubble. Swing kettle out of the direct fire to lower temperature and continue cooking at low heat, stirring occasionally, until apples are mushy (30 to 40 minutes.) Remove from heat. Discard cinnamon stick and let cool.

When cool, strain applesauce through a hand-cranked food mill (such as a Foley mill). Taste sauce and add additional sugar, if desired.

SERVES: 6 to 8
HEARTH COOKWARE: gypsy kettle with lid
FIRE: hot

8

Strategies for Planning a Fireplace Feast

In addition to its novelty, the pure fun of it, and the wonderful flavor it imparts to food, fireplace cooking and entertaining can be very compatible dinner partners. This is especially true if your fireplace is located in a family or living room, the usual home entertaining area. Cooking in the living room, as strange as it may sound, affords some real advantages for the cook and host or hostess. It resolves a common dilemma with which he or she is often faced: the choice of either laboring alone over final meal details in a separate kitchen, leaving guests to fend for themselves or with a spouse to entertain them; or having company wander into a hot, messy, and cramped dinner-party kitchen for a peek in the oven and a chat with the cook.

Picture instead: the soup gently simmering in the gypsy kettle, a bread or pie baking in the Dutch oven, and a roast browning before the fire on a spit. All supervised out of the corner of the chef's watchful eye, while the chef sits and enjoys a drink with the company. And, if an especially ambitious array of fireplace foods is planned, a guest is always near at hand, and more than willing, we have found, to turn the spit or baste the meat.

When dinner is completed, it can be served with great style directly from many of the unique open-hearth cooking pots and implements, cutting down on the use of serving platters to wash up later. For example, soup and other one-pot meals can be ladled directly from the interesting kettle in which they were cooked into individual bowls. A planked fish can be most strikingly presented, garnished, and brought to the table right on the rustic board on which it was roasted.

Second helpings, as well as dinner plates, are easily kept warm and at arm's reach at the fire's edge, eliminating the need for electric hot trays or a dash to the kitchen oven.

The energy savings possible with fireplace cooking also make it attractive for entertaining. Since many of us light a fire to make a room more inviting for guests, why not be thrifty as well, and use this heat to cook dinner for them, too?

And, a final word on its merits for entertaining: fireplace cooking is an intriguing performance for old friends and provides a great topic of conversation for new ones.

Practice fireplace cooking techniques and recipes on family before inviting company. The more complicated techniques or recipes may require a few trial runs before you feel completely comfortable with their execution and are satisfied with the results. While cooking in a fireplace is easy once you get the knack of it, the new skills and different tempo involved may seem awkward and even intimidating, at first, for the beginner.

Build up to five-course fireplace dinners slowly. Start with simple menus first, in which only one food is cooked in the fireplace and the rest are prepared ahead of time, preferably the night before, in your modern kitchen.

Set up your hearth cooking area before your guests arrive with all the equipment you're likely to need, to avoid countless trips to your regular kitchen for pot-holders, paper towels, serving platters, or carving knives.

Allow plenty of time for the food to cook. Open-hearth cooking times are not precise, but, since in general it takes slightly longer to cook food in your fireplace than with a modern appliance, we always have plenty of hors d'oeuvres on hand or serve a soup course to help hungry guests (and the cook) pass the time more patiently in case of a delay.

Keep in mind that no matter how proficient a fireplace chef you become, cooking for a large crowd on the open hearth may not be practical. Cooking food in large quantities in the fireplace can lose its novelty, and may become only hot, time-consuming, and a great deal of work. Even in our huge pre-Revolutionary walk-in hearth, we usually limit our fireplace dinners to eight, since most of the standard hearth cooking pots and implements have the capacity to cook only enough food to serve this number at one time.

On special occasions, when a large crowd is to be fed, we get around this problem by preparing a chili, or other substantial one-pot meal, in a gypsy kettle, a pot that is more readily found in the larger sizes, and accompany it with lots of extras fixed beforehand in our regular kitchens. And for a very festive occasion, if your fireplace is big enough, a professional restaurant spit can be rented to roast a suckling pig before the fire.

Finally, even though you're the hostess, don't lose sight of the fact that you're the chef, as well. Tending a fire and cooking with it can be a dirty, hot, and sometimes hazardous activity, especially in a fashionable hostess grown. So dress sensibly–Chapter 2, The Cooking Fire, discusses the appropriate apparel for fireplace cooking.

9

Where to Learn about Fireplace Cooking

Nothing quite matches the experience of learning a skill firsthand from an acknowledged expert. But since we can't bring back Eliza Leslie or Amelia Simmons to lecture on the art of fireplace cooking, we will direct you to the next best source, the many living history museums throughout the U.S. In these restored or re-created villages, plantations, farms, forts, and dwellings, fireplace cooking is practiced as it was in America's past. They span more than two hundred years from the earliest colonization of America, re-created at Plimoth Plantation, to later eras preserved at Hancock Shaker Village and the settling of the wild west. They recall a fascinating array of American lifestyles from the elegance and sophistication of Colonial Williamsburg to the simple farm setting of Old Sturbridge Village and the pioneer spirit of Missouri Town, 1855.

These museums use a "living history" format to portray the life and technology – cooking and manufacturing – of the different periods. Here, trained guides, often referred to as museum interpreters, reenact everyday tasks of the period. Dressed in period garments, they can be observed cooking fireplace meals with antique implements or faithful reproductions. Food indigenous to the region and menus reflecting the tastes and ethnic origins of its settlers are used in meal planning and preparation to create an overall effect that mirrors the past as faithfully as possible.

Hamburgers, hot dogs, and steaks won't be in evidence in these fireplace kitchens, although we encourage you to add these to your fireplace cooking repertoire. But one can get a good grasp on how to perform basic cooking techniques at your home hearth and with a bit of imagination, apply these skills to the preparation of fixin's more in keeping with 21st century tastes.

Holidays, especially Thanksgiving and Christmas, are very active and festive at living history sites and the occasion for the preparation of ambitious fireplace dinners characteristic of the festivities and customs of the season. And, when health codes permit, sometimes samples of the fireplace fare are offered to the public.

For a more hands-on experience, the larger and better-funded sites may offer special classes or workshops in fireplace cooking, especially during slower tourist months. A few such courses even carry college credit!

Following is a selection of living history sites throughout the U.S. where fireplace cooking is demonstrated and/or taught. Other places can be researched on the internet by "Google"-ing up Living History + Museums or the site for The Association for Living History Farms and Agricultural Museums, www.alhfam.org. Another useful internet site is www.preservation-history.com.

Connecticut

Mystic Seaport, 75 Greenmanville Avenue, P.O. Box 6000, Mystic, CT 06355-0990; 888-973-2787; www.mysticseaport.com; Through its adult education programs, Mystic Seaport offers open hearth cooking classes in the Buckingham-Hall House. Contact: Suzanne Reardon, 860-572-5323; suzannereardon@mysticseaport.org.

Indiana

Conner Prairie, 13400 Allisonville Road, Fishers, IN 46038-4499; 800-966-1836; www.connerprairie.org; Hearthside cooking classes.

Iowa

Living History Farms, 2600 111th Street, Urbandale, Iowa 50322; 515-278-5286; www.livinghistoryfarms.org; Open hearth cooking demonstrations and classes in pioneer hearth cooking at the 1850 Pioneer Farm.

Louisiana

Hermann-Grima/Gallier Historic Houses, 820 Saint Louis St., New Orleans, LA 70112; 504-525-5661; www.hgghh.org; Open hearth cooking demonstrations in the 1831 kitchen Thursdays, October through May, plus hands-on open hearth dinner classes for adults who cook then eat a meal of 19th century receipts.

Massachusetts

Old Sturbridge Village, 1 Old Sturbridge Village Road, Sturbridge, MA 01566; 800-733-1830; www.osv.org. Village life in the 1830s is recreated here. Educational opportunities include workshops in blacksmithing and other crafts.

Plimoth Plantation, 137 Warren Avenue, Plymouth, MA 02360; 508-746-1622; www.plimoth.org. The living history museum of the 17th century. Costumed role players portray English colonists of 1627 as they go about their daily lives in the Pilgrim Village. Experience harvest dinner with the pilgrims, a fall attraction.

Michigan

Biddle House, The; Market Street, Mackinac Island, MI 49757; 231-436-4219; www.MackinacParks.com; In the historic downtown, Biddle House hosts daily food preparation demonstrations in 18th century kitchen.

Colonial Michilimackinac, Mackinaw City, MI 49701; 231-436-4219; Fireplace cooking part of the 18th century village life interpretation.

Greenfield Village, The Henry Ford Museum, 20900 Oakwood Blvd. Dearborn, MI 48124-4088; 313-982-6001; www.thehenryford.org ; Fireplace cooking presented on a daily basis April 15 to January 1.

Missouri

Missouri Town 1855, 8010 East Park Road, Lee's Summit, MO 64015; 816-503-4860; www.jacksongov.org (link to recreation for Missouri Town 1855); Fireplace cooking workshops offered several times a year. Participants prepare the food and then enjoy it.

New Hampshire

Strawbery Banke, Marcy Street, Portsmouth, NH 03801; 603-433-1100; www.strawberybanke.org; Open hearth cooking every day in the Wheelwright House and periodic fireplace cooking workshops.

New Jersey

Historic Cold Spring Village, 720 Route 9, Cape May, NJ 08204; 609-898-2300; www.hcvs.org; Early to mid 19th century open hearth cooking demonstrated in Spicer Learning House during summer season.

New York

Farmer's Museum, The; 30 Lake Street, Cooperstown, NY 13326; 607-547-1450; www.farmersmuseum.org. 19th century open hearth cooking demonstrations daily, as well as occasional classes in fireplace cooking.

Historic Richmondtown, 441 Clarke Avenue, Staten Island, NY 10306; 718-351-1611; www.historicrichmondtown.org; 18th century open-hearth cooking demonstrations.

Old Bethpage Village Restoration, Round Swamp Road, Old Bethpage, NY 11804; 516-572-8400; www.oldbethpage.org; Fireplace and bake oven food preparation on weekends. Holiday cooking, including spit roasted turkey, around Thanksgiving.

North Carolina

Historic Latta Plantation, 5225 Sample Road, Huntersville, NC 28078; 704-875-2312; www.lattaplantation.org; Weekend demonstrations in summer kitchen and in slave cabin on 1800s plantation. Occasional classes in fireplace cooking for adults.

Old Salem, Winston-Salem, NC 27180; 888-653-7253; www.oldsalem.org. Living history town recreates the daily activities of the Moravians who settled Salem in 1766.

Ohio

Sauder Village, 22611 State Route 2, Archbold, Ohio 43502; 800-590-9755; www.saudervillage.org ; Native-American open fire cooking. Open hearth cooking to be offered.

Pennsylvania

Hope Lodge, 553 South Bethlehem Pike, Fort Washington, PA 19034; 215-646-1595; www.ushistory.org/hope ; Hands-on cooking workshops. Participants use replica cooking tools to prepare authentic foods and then enjoy them.

Landis Valley Museum, 2451 Kissel Hill road, Lancaster, PA 17601; 717-569-0401; www.landisvalleymuseum.org; Open hearth cooking demonstrated in the Tavern. Bake ovens fired for special events and classes in open-hearth cooking offered during summer and winter institutes.

Meadowcroft Museum of Rural Life, 401 Meadowcroft Road, Avella, PA 15312; 724-587-3412; www.pghhistory.org (link to Meadowcroft Museum); Fireplace cooking demonstrations on weekends and fall Harvest Supper immersion fireplace cooking experiences for small groups where participants prepare and savor the food they prepare over the open hearth.

Quiet Valley Living Historical Farm, 1000 Turkey Hill Road, Stroudsburg, PA 18360; 570-992-6161; www.quietvalley.org; Fireplace cooking demonstrations on Saturdays.

Texas

Dallas Heritage Village at Old City Park, 1717 Gano Street, Dallas, TX 75215; 214-421-5141; www.oldcitypark.org ; Open hearth cooking classes February through May and Late September through November.

Virginia

Colonial Williamsburg, Williamsburg, VA 23187; 757-229-1000; www.history.org. Click on foodways link for information on programs and resources on early American cooking. (Colonial Willamsburg is the world's largest living history museum.)

Frontier Culture Museum, 1290 Richmond Road, Staunton, VA 24401; 540-332-7850; www.frontier.virginia.gov; Fireplace cooking demonstrations (with hands-on interaction from visitors welcome) almost daily at the reconstructed German, Irish, English, and Appalachian farms at this site. Cooking classes offered occasionally.

Sources for Hearth Cookware and Accessories

In addition to the sources listed below, there are many, many working blacksmiths and tinsmiths throughout the country who can make almost any hearth cooking implement to your specifications. They can be resourced through the internet, through blacksmith and tinsmith associations, and through living history museums such as Sturbridge Village and Colonial Williamsburg. Particularly knowledgeable and authentic resources for handcrafted hearth cookware and accessories are Goosebay Workshops (specializes in 17th and 18th century copper, brass and tin) and Historic Housefitters. Both are listed below.

Baking Rings and Sheets

Goose Bay Workshops
10137 Seashore Highway
Bridgeville, DE   19933
302-337-8285
www.goosebay-workshops.com

Chestnut, Coffee, and Chocolate Roasters

Bridge Kitchenware Corporation
711 3rd Avenue
New York, NY   10017
212-688-4220
www.bridgekitchenware.com
8 and 24-inch handled chestnut roasters

Goose Bay Workshops
10137 Seashore Highway
Bridgeville, DE   19933
302-337-8285
www.goosebay-workshops.com
Copper bean roasters, coffee and chocolate

Cranes, Crane Hooks, Trammels, and Beehive Oven Doors

Ball and Ball
463 W. Lincoln Highway
Exton, PA   19341-2705
1-800-257-3711
www.ballandball-us.com

Historic Housefitters
P.O. Box 26
Brewster, NY   10509
1-800-247-4111
www.historichousefitters.com
Cranes, in stock and custom

Kayne and Son Custom Hardware
100 Daniel Ridge Road
Chandler, NC   28715
828-667-8868
www.customforgedhardware.com
Cranes, crane hooks, trammels,
bee hive oven doors

Old Smithy Shop
193A Route 13
Brookline, NH   03033
603-672-4113
www.oldsmithyshop.com
Cranes, crane hooks, trammels

SpitJack
1 Oak Hill Road
Worcester, MA   01609
1-800-755-5509
www.spitjack.com
Cranes, trammels

Dutch Ovens

Boy Scouts of America
Supply Division
National Distribution Center
P.O. Box 7143
Charlotte, NC   28241-7143
1-800-323-0732
www.scoutstuff.org
2, 6, 8, and 10 quart Dutch ovens
including a 14½-inch steel rod lid
lifter

Historic Housefitters
P.O. Box 26
Brewster, NY   10509
1-800-247-4111
www.historichousefitters.com
Camp and regular Dutch ovens in
two sizes and lid hooks

Lodge Manufacturing Co.
204 East Fifth Street
South Pittsburg, Tennessee   37380
423-837-7181
www.lodgemfg.com
Camp Dutch ovens in 2, 4, 6, 8,
10, and 12 quart sizes

MACA Supply Company
Springville, Utah
1-801-489-3663
www.macaovens.com
Extra-deep, extra-heavy, extra -
large camp Dutch ovens. Also in
oval shape for cooking chickens
and turkeys. (Can personalize
your oven lid with your name,
organization or other short
phrase.)

Plow & Hearth
1-800-494-7544
www.PlowAndHearth.com
4,6, and 8 quart Dutch ovens

Sims Stoves
P.O. Box 21405
Billings, MT   59104
1-800-736-5259
Lodge Manufacturing 2 to 12
quart capacity Dutch ovens

Gridirons, Toasters, Trivets

Historic Housefitters
P.O. Box 26
Brewster, NY   10509
1-800-247-4111
www.historichousefitters.com
Gridirons and trivets

Kayne and Son Custom Hardware
100 Daniel Ridge Road
Chandler, NC   28715
828-667-8868
www.customforgedhardware.com
Gridirons

Old Smithy Shop
193A Route 13
Brookline, NH   03033
603-672-4113
www.oldsmithyshop.com
Gridirons, toasters, trivets, skewers

Grills, All-Purpose and Fish

Boy Scouts of America
Supply Division
National Distribution Center
P.O. Box 7143
Charlotte, NC   28241-7143
1-800-323-0732
www.scoutstuff.org
Foldaway grill; and long-handled, non-stick, cast iron pie cooker that can also be used to toast sandwiches, grill chicken, and other foods.

Bridge Kitchenware Corporation
711 3rd Avenue
New York, New York   10017
212-688-4220
www.bridgekitchenware.com
Fish grills in numerous shapes and lengths for both whole fish and fillets from small sardines to a large 28-inch catch.

NapaStyle
574 Gateway Drive
Napa, CA   94558
1-866-776-6272
www.napastyle.com
A sturdy, all-purpose hearth grill (good for grilling meat, fish, veggies, etc.) that cantilevers out to hold shelf in place while you load or turn food. Adjustable, 3 level shelf, 17"x 17½" x 16"H. Wood handles.

SpitJack
1 Oak Hill Road
Worcester, MA   01609
1-800-755-5509
www.spitjack.com
Tuscan grills

Kettles and Kettle Lids

Goose Bay Workshops
10137 Seashore Highway
Bridgeville, DE   19933
302-337-8285
www.goosebay-workshops.com
Copper pots, both riveted and rolled; copper lids

Peels

Historic Housefitters
P.O. Box 26
Brewster, NY   10509
1-800-247-4111
www.historichousefitters.com
Iron, long handled

Pie and Hot Dog Irons

(Pie Irons can also be used to toast sandwiches, grill chicken, and other foods.)

Boy Scouts of America
Supply Division
National Distribution Center
P.O. Box 7143
Charlotte, NC   28241-7143
1-800-323-0732
www.scoutstuff.org
Long-handled, non-stick, cast iron pie cooker

Plow & Hearth
1-800-494-7544
www.PlowAndHearth.com
Pie and hot dog irons

Reflector Ovens (Tin Kitchens)

Boy Scouts of America
Supply Division
National Distribution Center
P.O. Box 7143
Charlotte, NC   28241-7143
1-800-323-0732
www.scoutstuff.org
Classic reflector oven (with 1 shelf)

Carl Giordano Tinsmith
PO Box 74
Wadsworth, Ohio   44282
www.cg-tinsmith.com
18th and 19th century reproduction tin ware

Historic Housefitters
P.O. Box 26
Brewster, NY   10509
1-800-247-4111
www.historichousefitters.com
Reproduction of 18th century tin kitchen with hand-forged spit and three skewers

Sims Stoves
P.O. Box 21405
Billings, MT   59104
1-800-736-5259
Single shelf, camp reflector ovens, 7 x 15 inches

Roasting Forks and Sticks

Boy Scouts of America
Supply Division
National Distribution Center
P.O. Box 7143
Charlotte, NC   28241-7143
1-800-323-0732
www.scoutstuff.org
41-inch long chrome-plated hot dog safety fork with a wooden handle that can also be used for grilling kebabs, etc.

Plow & Hearth
1-800-494-7544
www.PlowAndHearth.com
Roasting forks; reverse-tipped hot
dog sticks

Saucepans, Skillets, and Specialty Pans

Goose Bay Workshops
10137 Seashore Highway
Bridgeville, DE   19933
302-337-8285
www.goosebay-workshops.com
Long handled saucepan, brass
with tin lining; Dutch skillet, brass
with wood handle; and Poffertjes
pan, brass with wood handle.
(Poffertjes are pancake-donut like
treats. Recipe is included.)

Skewers

Historic Housefitters
P.O. Box 26
Brewster, NY   10509
1-800-247-4111
www.historichousefitters.com
Skewers with holder

Spiders (Spyders)

Goose Bay Workshops
10137 Seashore Highway
Bridgeville, DE   19933
302-337-8285
www.goosebay-workshops.com
Large and small brass pan spiders
with iron legs

Historic Housefitters
P.O. Box 26
Brewster, NY   10509
1-800-247-4111
www.historichousefitters.com
Spiders

Spit Jacks

Ball and Ball
463 W. Lincoln Highway
Exton, PA   19341-2705
1-800-257-3711
www.ballandball-us.com
Clockwork spit jacks

SpitJack
1 Oak Hill Road
Worcester, MA   01609
1-800-755-5509
www.spitjack.com
Electric and clockwork (wind up)
spit jacks. Optional drip pans and
accessories

Thermometers

Brookstone
1-866-576-7337
www.brookstone.com
BBQ fork thermometers are
handy for fireplace cooking.
Checks cooked temperature of
chicken, etc. Also quick-release
handle BBQ baskets that hold
multiple cuts of meat and veggies
for cooking without piercing.

Wood Grilling Planks

BBQWoods.com
P.O. Box 8163
Yakima, WA   98908
1-800-379-9663
www.bbqwoods.com
Variety pack of twelve 6 x 12
cooking planks includes Alder,
Cedar, Cherry, Hickory, Maple,
White Oak

Nature's Cuisine
1-866-880-4506
www.natures-cuisine.com
Cedar, Alder, Maple planks available separately or in variety sam-
pler or combo packs. Site also lists
retailers.

Sautee Cedar Company
328 Commerce Blvd., Unit 8
Bogart, GA   30622
866-728-8332
www.sauteecedar.com
Alder, Cedar, and Maple planks

Smith & Hawken
1-800-940-1170
www.smithandhawken.com
Grilling planks (15" x 7") in cedar
and maple infuse planked fish
and veggies with smoky flavor.
Sold in sets of 4.

Making Your Own Hearth Implements

For the inveterate do-it-yourselfer, here is a list of issues of *Early American Life* magazine that includes articles on making your own hearth cooking equipment. Published by the Early American Society, *Early American Life* is a popular magazine devoted to the understanding of American social history and modern interpretations of its early arts, crafts, furnishings, and architecture. Back issues of the magazine can be borrowed from public libraries that subscribe to *Early American Life*. Two of these articles—making a tin kitchen and a fireplace trivet—have been reprinted in *The Early American Fireplace Book,* recently published by the Society.

"Forging a Fireplace Toaster," *Early American Life*, February 1980
"Forging a Fireplace Trivet," *Early American Life*, April 1979
"Plans for a Tin Kitchen," *Early American Life*, October 1976.

And if you are really starting from scratch, two books, *The Forgotten Art of Building and Using a Brick Bake Oven*, by Richard M. Bacon, and *The Forgotten Art of Building a Good Fireplace*, by Vrest Orton, will be invaluable. Both are available from Alan C. Hood & Company, Inc., P.O. Box 775, Chambersburg, PA. 17201; www.hoodbooks.com

Equipping Your Fireplace with Antiques

Equipping your fireplace with antique cooking implements is by far the most expensive option for the fireplace cook, and is a pursuit unto itself. But, since some may want to consider this possibility—and since we are collectors ourselves—we felt it appropriate to give some observations on buying and using antiques for cooking before turning to more practical sources.

Antique dealers who specialize in early American kitchen equipment are a logical place to begin your search, but dealers who limit their stock exclusively to these items are few and far between. Most combine cooking pots and implements with other tools, such as those used for woodworking, blacksmithing, and tinsmithing. Most any dealer who favors early American primitives is likely to have an antique iron or tin cooking implement or two in his inventory. Don't be shocked by the prices! Rare examples of early American kitchen implements—a teakettle with a tilter, or spit andirons, for example—have been bid up to the $1200 price range at recent auctions, supposedly a wholesale source. When early pieces are signed by their makers, they command even higher prices. Good places to look for older, if not yet antique, implements at more reasonable prices are flea markets and even garage or tag sales. These sources can harbor real finds for the knowledgeable and lucky buyers.

Equipping your fireplace solely with antiques may turn out to be an unrealistically drawn-out and unpredictable process. Antiques are one of a kind, and, since a dealer's stock varies from month to month, the exact pot, trammel, or other accessory you are after may not be available precisely when you need it—or ever, for that matter, at a price you are willing to pay.

When buying antiques to use for actual cooking, you must be sure that they are in good condition or that it is possible to have them cleaned and restored to working order. Frequently, antique metal pots are painted or encrusted with rust, which must be removed before they can be used for preparing food. This can be done quite easily by professional metal strippers who use strong chemicals or sandblasting to clean the surfaces. But be wary of pieces that may be worn too thin or are too rusted to withstand the rigors of these methods. Also, avoid pots that have been converted to planters and have drainage holes drilled in their bottoms, and kettles with cracked or badly chipped enamel linings. These flaws cannot be mended. In general, though, most wrought iron and tin pieces can be repaired by a skilled blacksmith or tinsmith. Broken cast iron pieces are a little more difficult to fix, but we have had some success replaceing broken-off feet on these implements, as well.

Antique implements must also be handled with great care. Age and repeated exposure to the extreme temperatures of the fire have rendered their metals very brittle. Cracks appear, and small pieces snap off with the slightest provocation. A broken kettle foot, a cracked toaster, and a lost tin kitchen spout were just a few of the casualties our collections sustained while we were testing the recipes for this book.

Repairs are possible, as we just mentioned, but we are obligated to add that they do diminish the value of an antique object. And, while we love handling old pieces and cooking with them, we concede that they are perhaps best left to enhance the setting of your hearth. In fact, most restorations use only fine reproductions of antique cooking implements, made to their specifications or copied from originals in their collections, for fireplace cooking, a practice that preserves their true antiques for the enjoyment and education of future generations.

Appendix

The table below converts 18th and 19th century recipes, such as the ones that follow (found at the Lambertville, New Jersey flea market) to modern equivalents.

Pearl ash, the earliest powdered leavening agent, was discovered in America at the end of the 18th century. It is a crude form of potassium carbonate produced from wood ash. At the end of the 1700s some 8,000 tons of Pearl ash were exported to Europe. About 1850, Pearl ash was replaced by Saleratus (potassium bicarbonate).

These and other early American recipe ingredients, including isinglass (the first form of gelatin) can be ordered from www.deborahspantry.com.

Before Pearl ash, to make light cakes and other baked goods, beaten eggs and/or egg whites, yeast, or beer were the only leavening agents.

Soft Gingerbread

5 teacups flour, 2 of molasses, 2 of cream, 2 eggs
1 teaspoonful Pearl ash, 2 of ginger

Fruitcake

1 lb. flour, 1 lb. sugar, ½ lb. butter , 4 eggs
1 teacup of new milk, 1 teaspoonful of Saleratus, 1 lb raisins, 1 great
   spoonful of cloves, 1 do* of cinnamon, 3 loaves

*Do means ditto

Table of Equivalent Weights and Measures

Butter the size of an egg = ¼ cup
Butter the size of a walnut = 2 tablespoons
Coffee cup = 1 cup
Dessert spoon = 1½ teaspoons
Dram = ¾ teaspoon
Drops, 60 = ¾ teaspoon
Gill = ½ cup
Lump (e.g. of butter) = 2 tablespoons
Pound of eggs = 8 to 9 large
  (Colonial eggs were small, so cookbooks
   may suggest 10 to 12 per pound)
Pound of flour = about 3 to 3½ cups
  (Best to weigh if you have a scale)
Pound of sugar = 2 to 2½ cups
  (Again, best to weigh)
Salt spoon = ¼ teaspoon
Scruple = about ¼ teaspoon
  (This is an apothecary weight, 1/24 ounce)
Teacup = ¾ cup
Tin cup = 1 cup
Tumbler full = 2 cups
Wineglass (half a gill) = ¼ cup

Selected Bibliography

ANDERSON, JEAN. *Recipes from America's Restored Villages*. Garden City, New York: Doubleday & Company, Inc., 1975.*

ARESTY, ESTHER B. *The Delectable Past*. New York: Simon and Schuster, 1964.

BACON, RICHARD M. *The Forgotten Art of Building and Using a Brick Bake Oven*. Chambersburg, Pennsylvania: Alan C. Hood & Co., Inc., 1977.

BELOTE, JULIANNE. *The Compleat American Housewife 1776*. Concord, California: Nitty Gritty Productions, 1974.*

BOORSTIN, DANIEL J. *The Americans: The Colonial Experience*. New York: Random House, 1958.

BOOTH, LETHA and THE STAFF OF COLONIAL WILLIAMSBURG, compilers. *The Williamsburg Cookbook*. Williamsburg, Virginia: The Colonial Williamsburg Foundation, 1971.*

Boston Cookbook of 1883 (excerpts from), Wakefield, Massachusetts: Pride Publications, Inc., 1979

BRADLEY, MARTHA. *The British Housewife*. London, c. 1770.

BROOME COUNTY HISTORICAL SOCIETY. *The American Hearth, Colonial and Post-Colonial Cooking Tools*. Binghamton, New York: Roberson Center for the Arts and Sciences, 1976.

BULLOCK, HELEN. *The Williamsburg Art of Cookery*. Williamsburg, Virginia: The Colonial Williamsburg Foundation, 1939.*

CARSON, JANE. *Colonial Virginia Cookery*. Williamsburg, Virginia: The Colonial Williamsburg Foundation, 1968.

CARTER, SUSANNAH. *The Frugal Colonial Housewife.* Edited and illustrated by Jean McKibbin. Garden City, Long Island: Dolphin Books, Doubleday and Company, Inc.

CLUSELLS, SYLVAIN. *Cooking on Turning Spit & Grill.* Translated by Charles R. Liebman, London: Arthur Barker Limited, 1961.

COSENTINO, GERALDINE, and REGINA STEWART. *Kitchenware, A Golden Handbook of Collectibles.* New York: Golden Press, 1977.

DEMOS, JOHN. *A Little Commonwealth, Family Life in Plymouth Colony.* New York: Oxford University Press, 1970.

DONOVAN, MARY; HATRACK, AMY; MILLS, FRANCIS; and SHULL, ELIZABETH. *The Thirteen Colonies Cookbook.* New York: Praeger Publishers, Inc., 1975.*

EARLE, ALICE MORSE. *Home Life in Colonial Days.* New York: The Macmillan Company, 1898.

ELVERSON, VIRGINIA T., and MCLANAHAN, MARY. *A Cooking Legacy.* New York: Cornerstone Library, 1976.*

FARRINGTON, DORIS E *Fireside Cooks & Black Kettle Recipes.* Indianapolis and New York: The Bobbs-Merrill Company, 1976*

FEARS, J. WAYNE. *Backcountry Cooking.* Charlotte, North Carolina: Fast & Macmillan Publishers, Inc., 1980.

Food, Drink, and Recipes of Early New England. Sturbridge, Massachusetts: Old Sturbridge Village Booklet Series, 1963.*

FRANKLIN, LINDA CAMPBELL. *From Hearth to Cookstove.* Orlando, Florida: The House of Collectibles, Inc., 1978.

GLASSE, HANNAH. *The Art of Cookery Made Plain and Easy* (reprint of 1796 edition). Hamden, Connecticut: Archon Books, 1971.

GROW, LAWRENCE, Ed. *The Second Old House Catalogue.* New York: Universe Books, 1978.

HAAS, IRVIN. *America's Historic Villages & Restorations.* New York: Arco Publishing Company, Inc., 1974.

HALVERSON, DEBORAH G., Ed. *The Early American Life Fireplace Book.* Harrisburg, Pennsylvania: The Early American Society, 1980.

HARRIS, HESTER. *Cast Iron Cookbook.* Concord, California: Nitty Gritty Productions, 1969.

HARRISON, MOLLY. *The Kitchen In History*. New York: Charles Scribner's Sons, 1972.

HECHTLINGER, ADELAIDE. *The Seasonal Hearth, The Woman At Home In Early America*. Woodstock, New York: The Overlook Press, 1977.

HOLM, DON. *The Old-Fashioned Dutch Oven Cookbook*. Caldwell, Idaho: The Caxton Printers, Ltd., 1976.

JONES, EVAN. *American Food: The Gastronomic Story* (second edition). New York: Random House & Vintage Books, 1981.*

KAUFFMAN, HENRY J. *Early American Ironware, Cast and Wrought*. New York: Weathervane Books, 1966.

KAUFFMAN, HENRY J., and BOWERS, QUENTIN H. *Early American Andirons and Other Fireplace Accessories*. Nashville: Thomas Nelson, Inc., 1974.

LANTZ, LOUISE K. *Old American Kitchenware 1725-1925*. Nashville: Thomas Nelson, Inc.: and Hanover, Pennsylvania: Everybody's Press, 1970.

LARK, DAVID. *"Early American Kitchens,"* Gourmet (November 1969), pp. 17-19, 47-52.

LESLIE, ELIZA. *Directions for Cookery in its Various Branches* (reprint of 1848 edition). New York: The Arno Press Inc., 1973.

LECOQ, RAYMOND. *Les Objets de la Vie Domestique*. Paris: Berger-Levrault, 1979.

LYON, J. C. *The Fireplace Cook Book*. Santa Fe: Lightning Tree, 1975.

ORTON, VREST. *The Forgotten Art of Building a Good Fireplace*. Chambersburg, Pennsylvania: Alan C. Hood & Co., Inc., 1974.

PHIPPS, FRANCES. *Colonial Kitchens, Their Furnishings and Their Gardens*. New York: Hawthorn Books, Inc., 1972.

ROBERSON, JOHN and MARIE. *The Complete Barbecue Cookbook*. New York: Collier Books, 1967.

ROOT, WAVERLY, and DE ROCHEMONT, RICHARD. *Eating in America, A History*. New York: William Morrow & Company, Inc., 1976.

RAGSDALE, JOHN G. *Dutch Oven Cooking*. Houston: Pacesetter Press, 1973.

RANDOLPH, MARY. *The Virginia Housewife.* Philadelphia, 1855.
Restored Village Directory. 5th ed. New York: Quadrant Press, Inc., 1978.

ROWSOME, FRANK, JR. *The Bright and Glowing Place.* Brattleboro, Vermont: The Stephen Greene Press, 1975.

SZATHMARY, LOUIS. *American Gastronomy.* Chicago: Henry Regnery Company, 1974.*

SIMMONS, AMELIA. *American Cookery* (reprint of 1796 edition). Harriman, Tennessee: Pioneer Press, 1976.

TANNAHILL, REAY. *Food In History.* New York: Stein & Day, 1973.

*These volumes have been selected for the readers who wish to prepare an authentic early American feast in their fireplace. All of the books indicated contain either recipes or menus, or both, from primary sources, which have already been tested and adjusted to fit today's ingredients and measurements. Directions for preparing them with gas and electric appliances are also normally included. Most of these books can be readily found in a public library.

Also included in this list is *American Gastronomy*, by Louis Szathmary, which may be a little more difficult to locate on your local library shelves. It is well worth the search, though, if you are eager to try original recipes from some of the early cookbooks also included in this bibliography, now available in reprint editions, or recipes from other primary sources. Mr. Szathmary, a professional chef, restaurateur, and collector of rare cookbooks, devotes a whole chapter here to his excellent observations on how to translate antique recipes for use today. So, if you're ever confronted with a recipe which directs you to add one wine glass of sherry, or a gill of brandy to the cake batter, this is the place to begin!

Index